GREAT MASTERS

Acknowledgments
The publishers would like to thank the museums for reproduction permission and in particular the **Art Museum of the Ateneum** (The Central Art Archives), **Helsinki** for *Léopold Survage*. The publishers thank the **BRIDGEMAN ART LIBRARY** for their help in supplying the illustrations for the book.

Christie's, London: Woman in Blue; Boy with Red Hair; Head of a Woman; Portrait of Thora Klinchlowstrom; Seated Nude; Jean Hébuterne with White Collar; Jeanne Hébuterne.
Courtauld Institute Galleries, University of London: Seated Nude.
Galleria d'Arte Moderna, Milan: Portrait of Paul Guillaume.
Jesi collection, Milan: Man Leaning on a Table.
Metropolitan Museum of Art, New York: Juan Gris; Jacques Lipchitz and His Wife.
Museo de Arte, Sao Paulo: Self-Portrait.
Musée d'Art Moderne, Paris: Seated Nude with a Shirt; Portrait of Dedie (dedicated to Odette Hayden).
Pinacoteca di Brera, Milan: Head of Moïse Kisling.
Private collections: The Equestrienne (L'Amazone); La Belle Epicière; Girl in Blue Dress; Leopold Zborowski; Girl with Braids; Portrait of Franz Hellens.
Solomon R. Guggenheim Museum, New York: Nude with Necklace, her Eyes Closed; Yellow Sweater (Portrait of Mademoiselle Hébuterne).
William Young and Co., Boston: Head of a Woman Wearing a Hat .

Published by Park Lane
An imprint of Grange Books PLC
The Grange
Grange Yard
London SE1 3AG

This edition published 1994

ISBN 1 85627 557 4

Amedeo Modigliani

PARK
LANE

His Works

Amedeo Modigliani
His Life and Works

Amedeo Modigliani died when he was in his mid-thirties, but he left behind a unique body of work, including paintings and sculpture his contemporaries described as "totally different" and portraits and nudes so sensual that turn-of-the-century society proclaimed them "immoral." Today, almost one hundred years later, they are considered great works of art and a Modigliani can be easily identified on a museum wall.

The French art critic Jean Cassou said that "style is the greatest revelation of the art of Modigliani." And, indeed, when one thinks of a Modigliani, a very specific style is conjured up: The work is a portrait, usually of a woman, with elongated lines that animate the painting. The model is usually sitting, her position always graceful and languid, her expression one of dreamy melancholy. Her skin tones are luminous, intensely warm and glowing, accentuating her face with its almond eyes and small mouth, her elongated neck, arms, and hands. The background colors, the detail, and the clothes are of secondary importance. It is the person in the portrait, the startlingly real emotion, the glow that seems to come from within, the simple elegance of line and shape, that capture the viewer's attention and make Modigliani a great master.

But these easily recognized portraits, although among Modigiliani's finest work's, were painted late in his life. They are only one part of the series of great paintings and sculpture that he created in his short but prolific career.

Early Influences

Amedeo Modigliani was born in Leghorn, a city south of Rome, on July 12, 1884. He was the fourth and last child of a middle-class Jewish family. His grandparents had been wealthy Romans who enjoyed a cosmopolitan life in the city. Modigliani's grandfather, a banker, even lent money to a powerful cardinal, which led him erroneously to believe he had "friends in powerful places." He felt sufficiently strong and powerful himself to break an antiquated, prejudicial Italian law that forbade Jews to own property. When the officials learned of this, he was forced to give up all his real estate. Enraged, he packed up his entire family and moved to the country, to Leghorn, where he could live in peaceful prosperity.

Unfortunately, Amedeo's father, Flaminio, did not fare well in the countryside. He, too, became a banker, but by the time Modigliani was born, he had lost almost all his money and had begun to trade coal and hides to support his growing family.

Modigliani's mother, a spirited Frenchwoman from a family in Marseilles, refused to succumb to poverty's despair. While Flaminio passively accepted his failure, Eugenie steadfastly ignored it—and him. She opened an informal finishing school for girls in their house and single-handedly raised and educated her four children.

Eugenie played a pivotal role in Modigliani's career. He was her "baby"; she nursed him through his frequent bouts of pulmonary disease; she encouraged his talent. "Will he be an artist?" she wrote in her diary when Amedeo was quite young.

Amedeo continuously missed school at Leghorn because of his bad health. He had few childhood friends and spent a lot of time with his mother. Eugenie instilled in him a confident, aristocratic spirit, laced with strong ideals of social justice and tinged with her own *joie de vivre*.

Amedeo spent many days at home reading and fantasizing. As a result of his melancholy self-absorption, the novels and poetry he read, and the illness he constantly fought, he developed a romantic, mysterious, and decadent concept of life. On days when he felt well, instead of roughhousing with friends and sitting in a classroom learning the multiplication tables, Amedeo explored Leghorn's museums, sometimes in the company of his beloved grandfather. There he discovered the old masters, from Titian and Caravaggio to Dürer.

Modigliani loved Italy and Leghorn. As he wrote: "titter and chitter of swallows / over the Mediterranean / O Leghorn!" And yet, at the same time, he loathed the conservative lifestyle of his middle-class family. He hated the provincialism of the countryside. He loved his family and yet he wanted to escape, to explore the world and experience life. He loved the beauty and history of his city, and yet he wanted more, he needed more. He had to escape his landscape of conventionality, tradition, and illness. He had to live. This ambivalence, this love/hate affair with Italy, would haunt him throughout his life.

But this solitude did more than create restless yearnings. It gave him a chance to find himself—through art.

Recognizing her son's talent, Eugenie enrolled him in the painting classes at the Leghorn School of Fine Arts when he was only fourteen. But naturalism, as taught by Micheli, a pupil of the then-famous Italian painter Giovanni Fattori, did not inspire the boy. The rigid adherence to what is seen by the eye went completely against Modigliani's already unfolding predilection toward the romantic unknown, toward a new way of seeing in art and in life.

Leaving Home

In 1901, the seventeen-year-old Modigliani, afflicted still with respiratory problems, left Leghorn to travel and study art throughout Italy. He was impressed with Florence, with its art galleries and museums. In 1902, he settled there, enrolling in the School of Fine Arts only to leave a year later for a teaching position in Venice.

Venice . . . Florence . . . Capri . . . Naples. . . . The formal art education Modigliani had received could not compete with the innovations, the exuberance, he now witnessed. Here was a new perception, a new way of painting that was stylistic, symbolic, and interpretive. Here was an emphasis on vivid colors, splashes of contrasting paint, flat backgrounds—all very different from the rigidity of naturalism. This new way of painting grew out of a movement called Fauvism—a precursor to Cubism—which would lead the way to modern art.

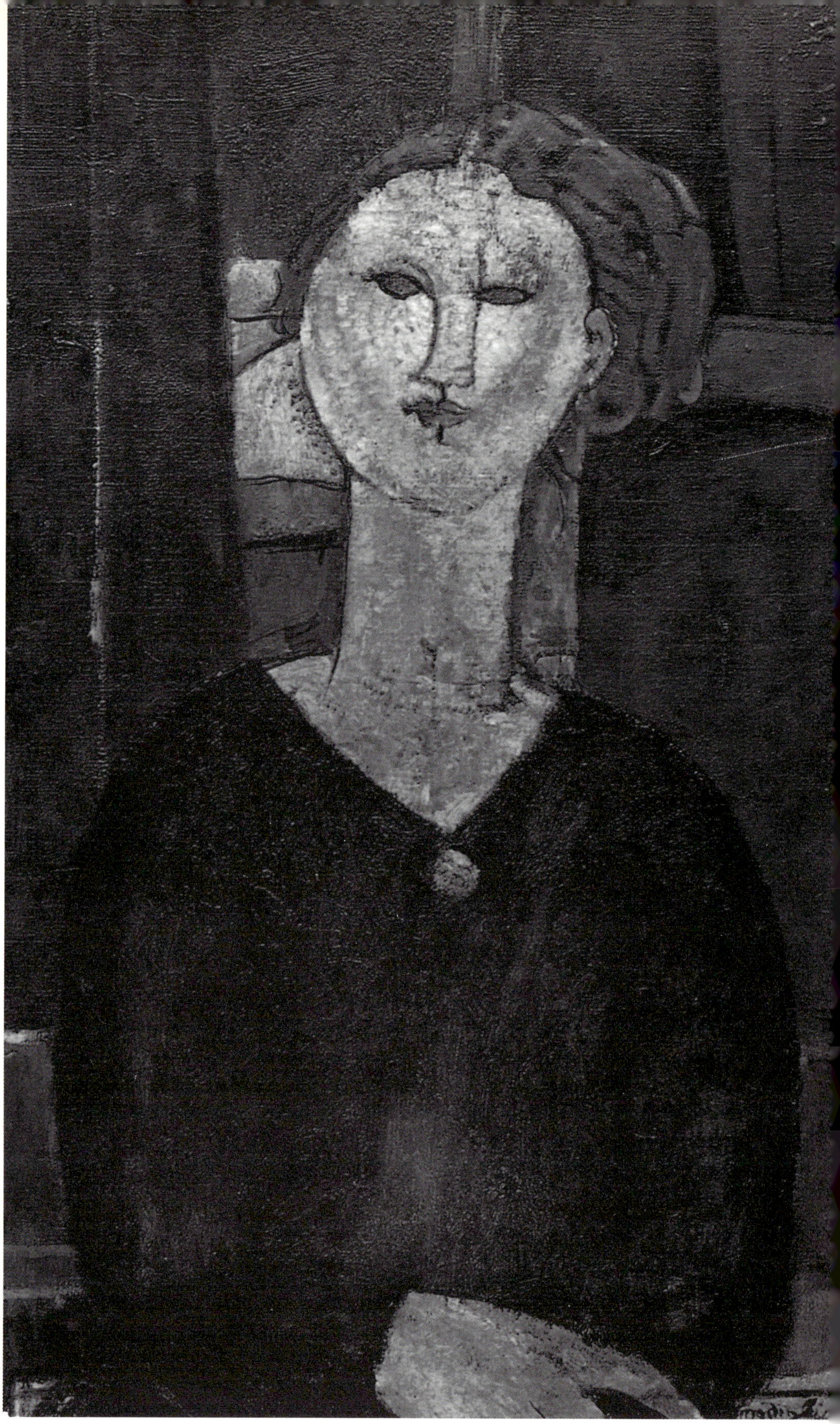

Antonia
(Detail)

Modigliani was also introduced to the sophistication and primitivism of African masks and Gothic arabesques, to the masters of medieval paintings and the Cubism that Cézanne was already turning into an art form. All this and more he saw, all this appealed to the sense of mystery, symbolism, and melodrama he first embraced as a sickly child at home.

At last, Modigliani found the inspiration he had been seeking, the way of seeing that was far removed from the naturalistic style of his school in Leghorn. He realized he was ready to grow and soar, to create a style that was all his own. And for anyone serious in art in those years, the place for that growth had to be Paris.

The Left Bank

Paris was the artistic capital of the world in the early part of the twentieth century. Modigliani was not the only young artist who dreamed of working and studying there. To Paris, in 1904, came Picasso, Brancusi, Pascin, and the painters Gris and Kandinsky. Two years later Modigliani arrived.

Just as there was only one city in Europe for artists, there was also only one place for Modigliani in Paris in those early days: Montmartre. Not only was it the area of Paris that welcomed the Impressionists with open arms at the Cafe Guerbois in the Boulevard Batignolles, but it was also the section of the city that offered van Gogh a brief resting place on his travels south—and inspired Toulouse-Lautrec at the Moulin Rouge he helped make legendary. Montmartre seemed the ideal spot for creative spirits to flourish in freedom—and that was exactly what Modigliani wanted. After his sojourn in the cities of Italy he craved an unfettered environment to develop his personality—unpersecuted, unencumbered, and completely free.

It would be a serendipitous move. The influences of the Italian Renaissance masters, the medieval paintings, and the primitive sculptures he studied would now mingle with the wild and varied stimuli of the contemporary Paris. The result of this creative union would be a legacy of paintings and sculpture of singular beauty and emotion.

At this point, Modigliani already displayed a "master of his own fate" attitude in his art. He had always had confidence in his abilities. He knew what he wanted to do in his art ever since he had started art school. It was this steadfast confidence in himself as an artist that enabled him to resist the powerful creative influences that permeated Paris at this time—especially the powerful appeal of Cubism. While Picasso, inspired by the austere simplicity of African art, worked at the studio Bateau-Lavoir, making Cubism an art form with his famous *Demoiselles d'Avignon*, Modigliani simply turned away. He would use some of the techniques of Picasso's Cubism, but only when his style was already intact. His bow to this aesthetic and technical revolution in style can be seen in the stark, superficial geometrical lines he used to construct some of his paintings, particularly in the way he segmented and separated their backgrounds. In *Antonia*, one of his early portraits, for example, the Cubist influence is evident, but only as one aspect of Modigliani's inimitable style.

He had absolutely no interest in painting the world around him. He rejected the style of his good friend and drinking companion Maurice Utrillo, who was to make famous picturesque scenes of village streets. And he rejected the vivid colors and flat perspectives of the Fauves' landscapes—which, when he was studying in Italy, had first showed him the possibilities beyond the naturalistic approach he had been taught. By 1906, Fauvism had grown popular in Paris. Showing landscapes from van Gogh and Gauguin, the movement caused a scandal at the art establishment's 1906 Salon d'Automne exhibit. Although embraced by avant-garde artists, Modigliani turned away, unmoved.

Modigliani was also against the anti-traditional principles of Italian Futurism, which scorned nature while glorifying the modern world, its automobiles, machinery, and simultaneous movement. The Futurists wanted to rid the world of everything old—including the nudes, the statues, and the centuries-old great works of the Italian masters. In the "Manifesto of Futurist Painting," they outlined their vilification of all things Italian, "the land of the dead." Gino Severini, a famous Futuristic painter, invited his compatriot Modigliani to subscribe to the ideals of this manifesto when it was published on February 11, 1911. But by then Modigliani's own style was nearly intact and he refused.

The Positive Influences

Modigliani did not reject everything he saw. There were artistic innovations that influenced his work. While he worked on developing his own forms and techniques, undecided and unsure of his ultimate direction, Modigliani hung reproductions of the paintings of the medieval and Renaissance masters on his studio walls. As he paused in a brushstroke, adding a splash of color to one of his portraits, perhaps he looked up at these prints and received inspiration from their luminous glow, their plays of light and dark, their symbolic arabesques.

By 1907, Modigliani had produced enough work to be accepted as a member of the artistic Société des Indépendants. It was also the year he was introduced to the work of Cézanne. A Cézanne memorial exhibition, on the first anniversary of the artist's death, was shown at the Salon d'Automne and greatly impressed Modigliani. For the first time, he embraced a contemporary artist. No longer did he stay with the past, with his Italian great masters, his primitive masks, his medieval gothic arabesques.

Modigliani overtly incorporated Cézanne's bold use of separation, of perspective and shape, of color into his own palette and into his style.

Cézanne's influence appeared almost immediately in Modigliani's work, in the strokes of color he used in *La Juive* in 1908, in the vivid portrait of Constantino Brancusi that he painted on the back of a sketch he would later use for *Cellist* in 1909, and in his *Portrait of Henry Laurens.*

But nowhere is Cézanne's influence revealed more than in Modigliani's *Beggar of Leghorn*, completed in 1909. An adaptation of a seventeenth-century Neapolitan picture, its bold lines, stark background, and colors inspired his daughter, Jeanne, to later call it a "watered-down Cézannesque structure." Although Modigliani eventually darkened the background and softened the features of the beggar, including his short hair, unseeing eyes, crooked nose, and long mustache, Cézanne's influence could still be discerned.

Using Cézanne's techniques was not a complete change of face for Modigliani. Actually, Cézanne's style, with its strict composition and shading, did not deviate too much from the training Modigliani received at Leghorn and throughout Italy. Nor did

Modigliani simply and passively adapt Cézanne. He was a young artist in search of new directions; he needed to find artistic currents that satisfied his already well-defined painterly inclinations—and Cézanne fit the bill for a while.

Eventually, however, Modigliani also left the world of Cézanne—and of French painting. He ultimately found its pure pictorial approach and its absence of emotional undertones incompatible with the humanistic, intellectual concepts he had embraced long ago in Italy, on Tuscan soil and within his Jewish family. After all, Modigliani was born Italian; he did receive a classical art education in Italy. He could not escape his origins—nor would he try. Instead, he continued to search, trying on one style, rejecting another, but always coming back to a classical foundation.

Paris, in these early years of the new century, was indeed the place to search for artistic, intellectual, and philosophical meaning, for new, unfettered innovations. But Paris was also a place where decadence could be romanticized, where soulful angst could be deified, where any behavior was condoned in the name of art.

This, too, appealed to the young, intense, and handsome Modigliani.

A Darker Side

In addition to discussions of his brilliant work, Modigliani's admirers also mention his famous self-destruction. His alcoholism, his addiction to hashish and other drugs, his short-lived relationships, his instability, and his unhealthy sleeping and eating habits had been described and analyzed as well. Indeed, his colleagues and critics agree that Modigliani's decadence seemed to become a preoccupation, a "death-wish" to exhaust his potential in only a few years. Although much has been written about these negative aspects of Modigliani's life, the excesses, the drunken bouts, the drugs, and the erratic, impulse behavior, some of the scandals are exaggerated and Modigliani himself, with his handsome, melancholy face and feverish, haunted eyes, created his own aura of mystery.

Modigliani's excesses could at times also be joyful and amusing. When, for example, the sculptor Jacques Lipchitz was introduced to Modigliani by the poet Max Jacobs, they were in the very public

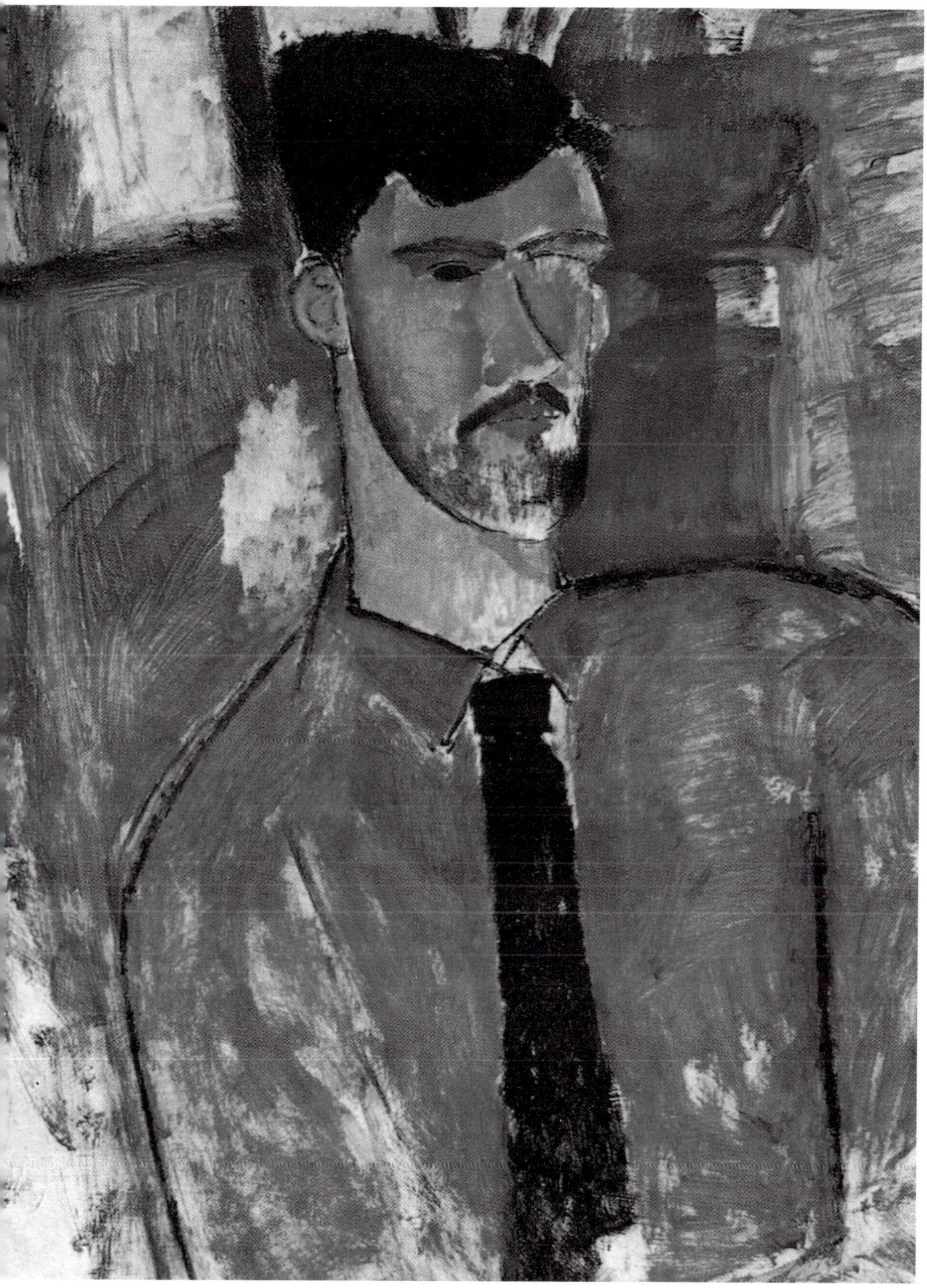

Portrait of Henry Laurens
(Detail)

Luxemburg Gardens. No sooner was Modigliani introduced than he launched into an eloquent rendition of the *Divine Comedy*. Although Lipchitz could not understand a word of it, he was totally entranced by Modigliani's exuberance. Lipchitz was not alone. Modigliani was always a welcome and entertaining friend among his Parisian colleagues.

But regardless of his excesses and the vicissitudes of his life, Modigliani's work, as with any great artist, stands alone. And Modigliani created works of stylistic perfection that held no clue to the torment of the man within. As art historian Jacques Lassasigne wrote, "The excesses of his life were none other than different manifestations of his unmitigated and fanatical dedication to the artistic adventure."

Claude Roy, in his biography of Modigliani, suggests that the progressive dissolution of the artist's life reflected the exact opposite of the stylistic evolution of his work, that "whilst he furiously destroyed the fabric of his existence with extreme perseverance, he patiently constructed the fabric of his genius with rigorous discipline." In other words, Modigliani's discipline went completely into his work. There was nothing left for life.

Beginning Portraits

In the fall of 1908, Modigliani met Dr. Paul Alexandre, an art collector who became a close friend. He would also be one of the first people to sit for Modigliani, to help him develop his portrait paintings into a fine art.

Together, Modigliani and Alexandre roamed the streets of Paris, visiting galleries that exhibited the works of Cézanne, Matisse, and Toulouse-Lautrec, browsing in antique shops and meeting with art dealers. With Alexandre at his side, Modigliani would stop and stare at the primitive African masks that also so appealed to Picasso, the masks that, when combined with Modigliani's love of the human face and body, would help him create a unique art form in portraiture.

Dr. Alexandre sat for Modigliani on three occasions. The first portrait showed the artist's classical knowledge and skills, as well as his ability to make his subject simultaneously elegant, compelling, and real. It was this raw talent, this innate ability to translate and transpose his subjects, that could have made Modigliani one of the most famous portrait painters in Paris, as well as a wealthy one. He could have rivaled his fellow countryman Giovanni Boldini, a fashionable artist in Paris, whose work Modigliani held in high esteem.

But it could never be. Modigliani would never be able to work for others. Although he had a passion for portraiture, it was on his terms and on his whim. He liked to use as models his friends and people who lived in his neighborhood. He liked to be spontaneous, to follow the spirit of the moment, and his proud, independent, and at times aggressive nature would never allow him to submit to the "slavery" of working on commission.

Above all, however, there was nothing that could divert him from his real aim: to become aware, to conquer his repressed fears, his rage, and his passion, and, ultimately, attain his own artistic truths. Working on commission could never give Modigliani the chance to get close to his soul. To remain true to his art, he had to remain true to himself.

By 1909, Modigliani had almost reached his goal, particularly in his drawings.

Drawing Skills

Modigliani drew constantly, a daily exercise that spontaneously allowed him to develop the familiar style of his maturity with its bold outlines and its unique, almost organic, composition. But his prolific drawing was not just a passion. It was a way to survive or, at the very least, a way to procure the glasses of alcohol that would become indispensable to him. Modigliani never went to one of the local cafés without a sketch pad and pencil, in search of a likely customer.

The painter Gabriel Fournier frequently witnessed these scenes and describes them in his memoirs: "Once he had found the friend he seemed to be looking for, he would approach him as if attracted by some particular feature, sit down at the corner of the table, open his sketch pad and caress the page with his hand. Then he would gaze sternly and deeply into the eyes of the chosen sitter, who seemed almost hypnotized. Then his pencil would fly in all directions over the page, and the artist would become very calm, singing away quietly to himself. He sketched a rapid series of arabesques, and then stopped suddenly, stroked the paper with the palm of his hand and concentrated his furious efforts on some small detail. If he was not satisfied with his first attempt, he would reject it with an air of absolute indifference and look around him before throwing himself upon a new sheet of paper, attacking it with violence. And then, moving his head even further back, he would sign the sketch with nonchalance before offering it to the sitter in exchange for a glass of gin. And then he left."

The many drawings Modigliani created enhanced his technical skills. They honed his keen powers of observation and his ability to work rapidly. The result was a marvelous ability to recognize the essence of a feature, an expression, or posture, an essence that, eventually, would come into play in the economy and breath of his mature, and greatest, paintings. His drawings show his talent to endow his lines with heightened sensitivity. He did not use pencil strokes to physically construct the contours of a figure. Instead, he managed to embrace the overall form by merely suggesting its shape.

It was the primary focus of Modigliani's lines that made his work different from that of his contemporaries. He combined these simple, suggestive lines with the classic ideal of medieval beauty he had embraced early on in Italy to create a unique and absolute modern stance. This can be seen in his portrait *Woman with a Black Neck Tie*.

There is another rather pragmatic reason why critics and historians explore Modigliani's drawings. Although Modigliani left a great many drawings from his time in Montmartre, there are few paintings intact. His private demons, his misgivings and dissatisfactions often led him to leave his paintings unfinished, abandoning them in his frequent moves from apartment to apartment, or even destroying them in the furious attacks of rage that often affected him when he was drunk. Modigliani was also known to destroy his work after the stultifying effects of the hashish that he had smoked began to wear off.

Modigliani's lifestyle was beginning to interfere with his art.

Leaving Montmartre

In 1909, Montparnasse was considered a lower-middle-class suburb of Paris; it was not yet an international center for the arts. But for Modigliani, short of money, it seemed a haven. It was inexpensive and, best of all, it had wonderful studio space. Artists' studios clustered in buildings and neighborhoods, brightened by tiny parks and the convenience of living in Paris. It was here, in Montparnasse, where the famous Café de la Rotonde stood opposite the equally famous Café de la Dome, where the Rive Gauche became synonymous with style, where the great Eastern European artists migrated to study and work. Montparnasse was stimulating and exciting. Many artists, including Matisse, Derain, Léger, Laurens, and Delaunay, worked side by side, creating paintings and sculpture that contributed to the growing fame of this quarter of Paris.

In 1909, Modigliani decided to move to Montparnasse, where he would live until his death. The move signaled an important change in his inclinations and in his art. He found a kinship among the Eastern European refugees who flocked to Montparnasse. He grew closer to them than he had ever been to his colleagues in Montmartre. There he would discuss art and politics in Lipchitz's studio. There at night, at the Dome or the Rotonde, he would drink, smoke, and talk with such artists as Pascin, Kisling, and Soutine, all the while sketching portraits of customers on napkins. Together, this Montparnesse group made up the Paris School, which was characterized by the foreign artists working in the city, each in search of his own particular style.

It was here, in the comfortable and nurturing surroundings of Montparnesse in 1909, that Modigliani decided to try sculpture, influenced by his new friend the Rumanian sculptor Constanin Brancusi.

Stylized Sculpture

By the time Modigliani met Brancusi, the sculptor had been living in Montparnasse for five years and lived in a studio also occupied by the avant-garde poet Guillaume Apollinaire, the poet Max Jacob, and the primitive painter Henri Rousseau.

Modigliani showed Brancusi some of his drawings. When Brancusi saw the drawings of female sculpted columns, called caryatids, and the sketches of stylized female heads, he felt they would successfully translate into stone and encouraged Modigliani to learn how to carve stone. He taught him the basics.

Within a year, Modigliani had rented a small studio at the Cité Falguière where he could sculpt. Sculpting became his passion. Indeed, many of Modigliani's first friends in Montparnasse knew him only as a sculptor; they had no idea that he had been trained to paint.

Money was always a problem for the struggling Modigliani, especially with the high cost of stone and sculpting materials. His debilitating lifestyle was also having a deleterious effect. Modigliani needed a rest, and in the autumn of 1909, he went to Leghorn for a visit.

During his stay, Modigliani supposedly did a number of sculptures in the famed Carrara marble that Michelangelo had used for his masterpieces. Unfortunately, the extent of the actual work Modigliani did that autumn in Leghorn will never be known. One night, near the end of his visit, in a drunken fit he threw all the statues he had been working on into a Leghorn canal. They are supposedly there still, silent and buried.

Modigliani's sculpting did not, however, end with the "drowning." Refreshed from his trip, he continued sculpting with renewed zeal in his small Montparnasse studio.

Sculpting freed Modigliani from the realist tradition in which he had been trained. It allowed him to explore and exploit the many different influences in Paris that he had spurned in his painting. Here, for the taking, was the originality of Cézanne, the daring creations of the French modernist painters, the stimulation of Cubism and the mystical primitiveness of African art, the rough brushstrokes and abstract lines of Expressionism—all now seen in a different perspective without the confines of canvas. Like a dancer rigorously trained in classical ballet who suddenly discovers the unencumbered freedom of modern dance, Modigliani the sculptor approached his new medium without any preconceived notions, only an open-minded confidence and enthusiasm.

Ultimately, however, Modigliani's passion for sculpting diminished. In *Montparnasse Vivant*, J.P. Crespelle wrote, "It is probable

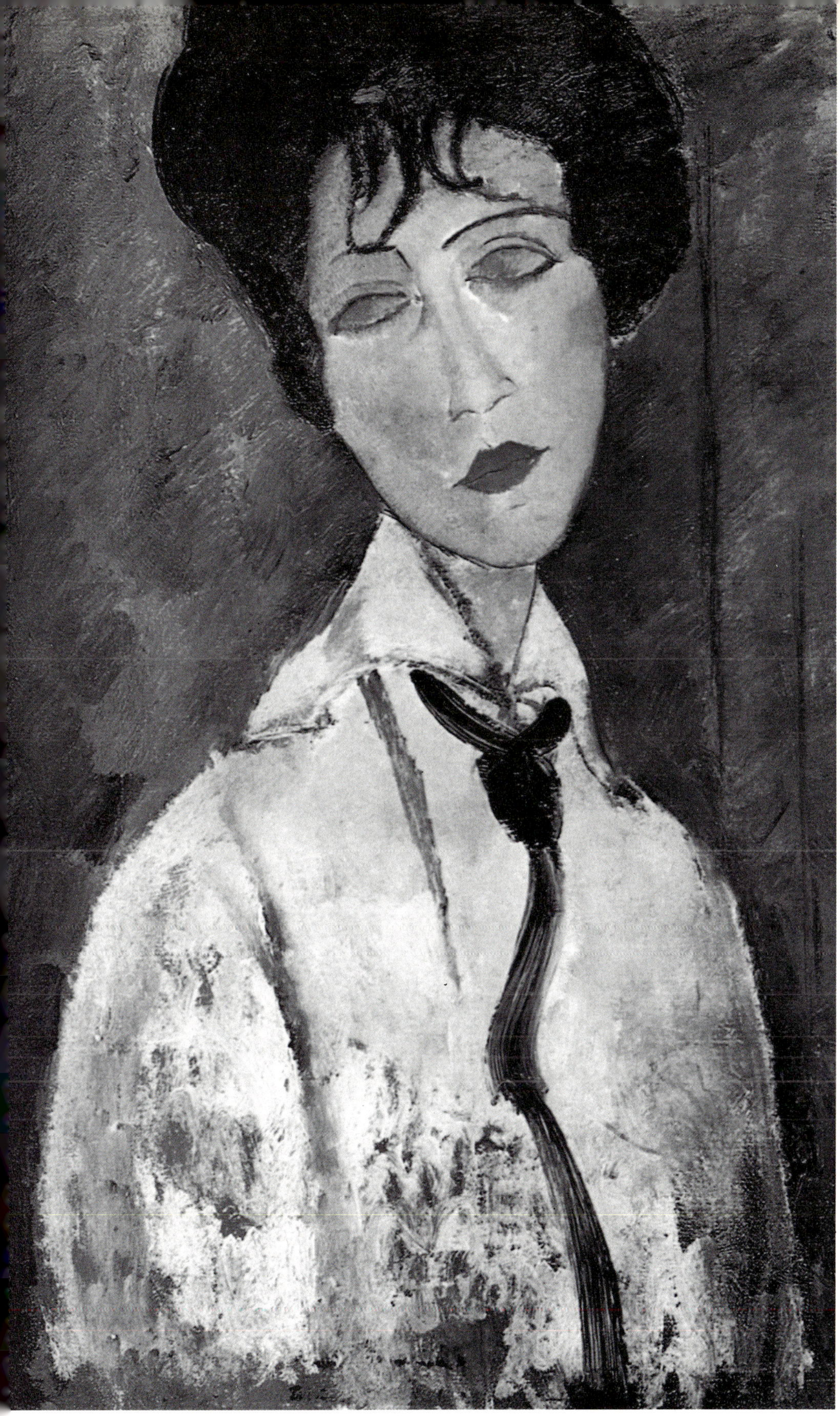

Woman with a Black Necktie (Detail)

that in this period Modigliani intended to dedicate himself to sculpture, and that purely material difficulties, such as the lack of money with which to buy blocks of stone, and the impossibility of reconciling the permanence implicit in the practice of sculpture with the temporary nature of the interminable series of places in which he lived, forced him to discontinue his project. Furthermore, the art of sculpture requires qualities of patience and self-control that were certainly not a part of Modigliani's character, who was prone to a feverish desire to express himself and complete his works rapidly."

The Road Back to Painting

Modigliani's family was supportive of his work. They not only welcomed him back to Leghorn whenever he visited, but when he was in Paris they sent him whatever money they could. Unfortunately, in 1914, the outbreak of World War I cut off even this meager income. Desperate for money, Modigliani would spend his daylight hours at the Rotonde, feverishly drawing portraits of customers while they sat and ate. After working hard all day to earn what he needed for supplies, he would return to his studio and sculpt. But it was difficult and Modigliani was forced to give up his studio space at Cité Falguière and began working at the studios of friends.

The outbreak of the war brought another kind of despair to the poverty-stricken artist. It also meant loneliness. Most of his friends had either been called up or enlisted. Although Modigliani might also have wanted to serve, his precarious health made it impossible. Thus he was left virtually alone in Paris, a city suddenly faced with far more pressing concerns than art and the lives of artists.

Then in 1914 he met the English poet Beatrice Hastings. She became the model for many of his works. They began an affair and she offered him solace and made his life less hard. But even with Beatrice's help, Modigliani's work became sporadic during this difficult year, until he met Leopold Zborowski, the Polish poet and art dealer. They became close friends. Zborowski was there to offer support, to encourage him, and to assist him financially. Powerful and positive, he encouraged Modigliani to return to painting as did the French art dealer Paul Guillaume. One day Guillaume entered the Rotonde and Modigliani's friend Max Jacob noticed him. Jacob pushed Modigliani to show his drawings to the dealer. At first, Modigliani refused. Finally, he begrudgingly went over to Guillaume's table. The art dealer was intriguedand he asked to see a painting. Poor and frustrated, Modigliani felt he had no choice. He had to begin painting again. By 1915, Modigliani was painting—exclusively.

Modigliani's dedication to sculpture and drawing before turning seriously to painting proved prophetic. Because he had experimented in different directions, he was able to discover a mature painting style that is immediately recognizable and composed with the genius his early work only promised.

Modigliani's new painting style can be seen in *Jacques Lipchitz and His Wife*. Despite the softness of the curve that follows the silhouette of the figures, there is a boldness to it, a unique curvature of line and form. Here is the influence of Expressionism in its construction, in its bold use of color, its contrasting shapes, its emotional, almost abstract quality.

Modigliani's 1916 *Max Jacob with Hat*, with its firmly designed face and realistic rendering of the features, shows the influence of Cubism's geometric style, but with a difference. With his fluid lines and forms, he adapted the Cubists' techniques not only for the model, but for the entire composition.

The influence of the years Modigliani spent as a sculptor can also be seen in his mature paintings. In his 1917 portrait of *Marcella*, for example, he directly transposed the features and forms of his stone heads into a precise pictorial interpretation. The elongated oval of the face is emphasized by a prominent nose. The neck has the strength of a caryatid, a supporting stone column.

Without question after 1915 Modigliani's style was becoming clear. His loose construction and his fluid lines, his use of earthy colors applied in broad brushstrokes, his geometric, asymmetrical composition—all these elements were coming together. And, indeed, beginning in 1915, Modigliani's production steadily increased. In less than five years, he produced more than three hundred paintings, all of them of the same high quality.

But Modigliani's work was selling only sporadically. And his life itself was spinning out of control.

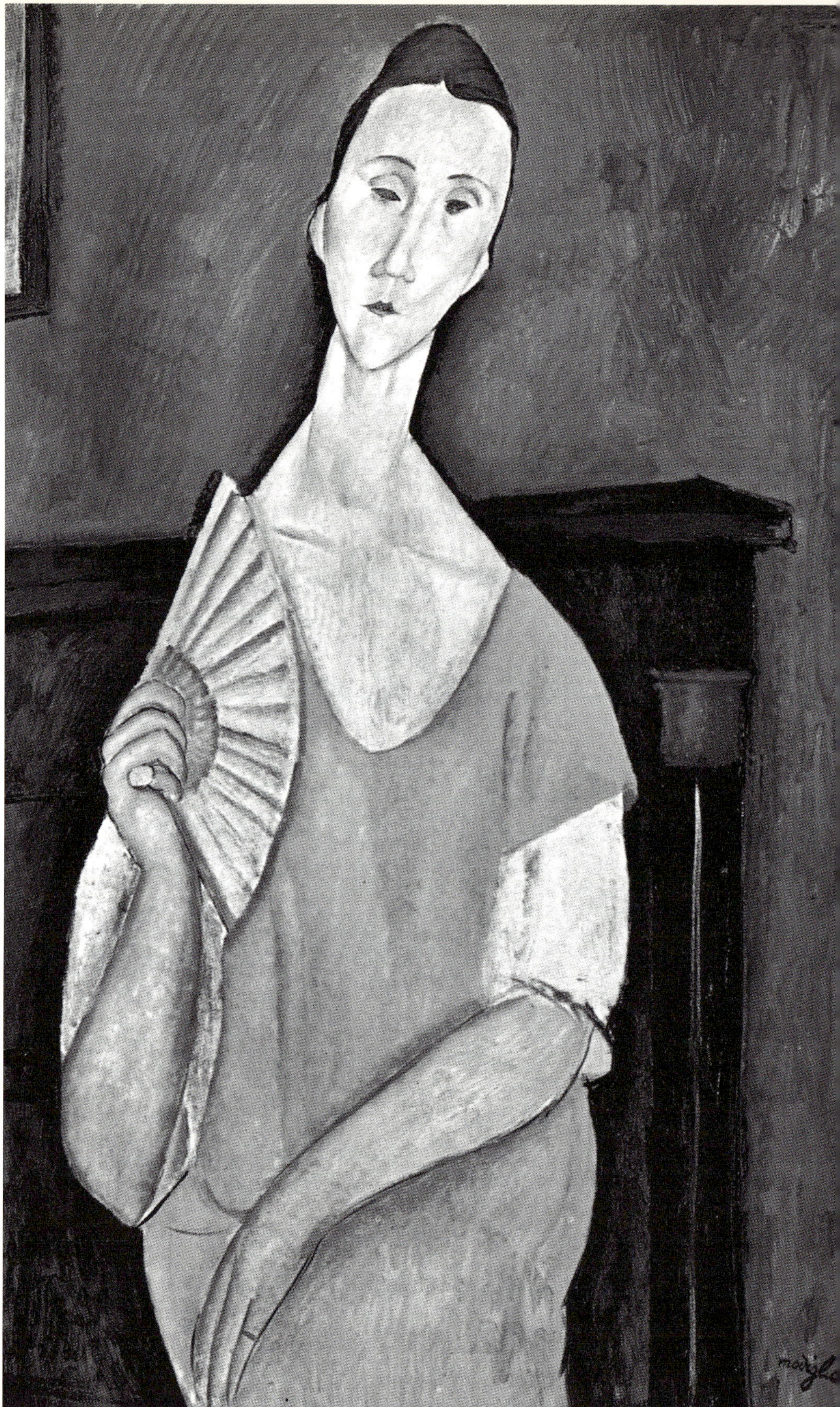

Lunia Czechowska with a Fan

Meeting Jeanne

When Modigliani met the nineteen-year-old chestnut-haired, blue-eyed Jeanne Hébuterne, his life began to change. Although he was fourteen years her senior, Modigliani was still youthful, bold, and handsome, and Jeanne was immediately drawn to him. Their love affair began in July 1917. They moved in together, living in a seedy hotel, with the complete disapproval of the conservative and Catholic Hébuterne family.

But the couple were madly and passionately in love. At last, Modigliani found the inspiration that would make him great. At last, he had a focus. Indeed, he painted Jeanne twenty-five times.

Jeanne was the love of his life. She was the only woman who could presume to seek him out when he stayed out late with his friends. She would find him when the cafés were closed, slumped in a chair. She would quietly say, "Let's go home, Amedeo." Slowly, he would get up and, arm in arm, they would leave.

So strong and solid was their relationship that Zborowski, their mutual friend, hoped that, at last, Modigliani would settle down and curb his excesses. He didn't. But although the drunken nights and fits of rage continued, Modigliani and Jeanne remained together for the rest of his life.

Analyzing Perfection

With Jeanne as inspiration and comfort, Modigliani was able to bring his art to great heights, combining his background in drawing, sculpting, and classical painting to create masterpieces of seemingly simple perfection. Indeed, at first glance, a Modigliani painting might almost seem haphazard, a series of lines and shapes that somehow evoke a magical quality. But his work was never unconscious.

Although his initial inspiration might have been spontaneous, Modigliani used a specific construction and detail in every one of his canvases. Each of his paintings is solidly assembled and perfectly balanced. The seated figures, for example, are a study in organization. The perpendicular posture of his seated models offers a pleasing and stable contrast to the inclination of the heads and the movement of the arms. Even his reclining nudes, with their sinuous curves and countercurves, are organized around an oblique axis stretching across the composition.

The portrait *Lunia Czechowska with a Fan* exemplifies the stability and the careful organization of Modigliani's seemingly weightless poses. All the lines composing the painting are enclosed within an oval that ends toward the bottom of the picture.

In *Jeanne Hébuterne Leaning on a Chair* (1918), the rigorous pose is less pronounced. Here, the asymmetric lines create a carefully calculated rhythm of gestures that, as a whole, provide equilibrium to the overall composition.

Indeed, lines were everything to Modigliani. His style was based on linear techniques; it is his lines that provide the principal source of overall clarity. His subject is immediately recognized not only by a few carefully placed lines and curves, but by the highly sensitive nuances that, translated onto canvas, totally express the most subtle of the artist's emotions.

Modigliani's style was further enhanced by the parsimony with which he used other painting techniques. His paint, for example, became lighter as he worked, as the brushwork, initially coarse and rough, was softened and the colors made more refined and blurred. Like his great medieval predecessors, he remained faithful to the physical truth of his model by keeping his style simple. Like them, his palette was quite somber; he used only soft, less penetrating colors. Ochres, earthy browns, grays, reds, greens, dull blues, heavy black, and white were all he needed to convey the subtlety of flesh and clothing and to construct his stylized backgrounds, which, like their medieval roots, were sparse.

Unlike classical paintings, however, Modigliani often divided his backgrounds into two vertical zones of neutral shades, which made his sharply outlined figure stand out. The result was a unique and perfect harmony between background and subject, and a highly contemporary work.

By combining the freedom and insight of modern expression with the rigor of traditional canons, Modigliani created a unique style, one that has won him a universally recognized prominence among the painters who worked and lived in Paris during this golden age of art.

The Great Portraits

But there is more than linear construction and singular style to make a Modigliani painting great. There is also emotion, the essence of life. Painting gave Modigliani the opportunity to enter other peoples' lives, to get to know them intimately by studying them, by evoking their presence on the canvas. To that end, he let his models' personalities take over. He became the subordinate, the chameleon, adapting his technical approaches, manner, and style to their physical and psychological characteristics.

This relationship between model and artist also provides a record of the significant events and people in Modigliani's life. Here, in the faces of his models, are Modigliani's attachments, his few true friends, his many casual acquaintances, his brief affairs, and his deep love for Jeanne. Here, in this veritable portrait gallery, we find the men and women who played roles in Modigliani's life, those closest to him and those he met only once or twice.

The models in his paintings hold another key to the growth of the man as an artist. They correspond to the phases in his development, ultimately leading to the perfection of his distinctive style. In the early years, Modigliani's work consisted of portraits of his companions in Montmartre and Montparnasse; they reflected Cézanne and other artists of the time. Here were his colleagues, Picasso, Jacob, and Dr. Alexandre. All the while, in these portraits, Modigliani was honing his techniques and style into his unique reflection of the human soul, capturing an essence and illuminating it with an asymmetrical line, a brush of color, a slope of shoulder, a turn of the head, a hand held just so on a lap.

Eventually, after 1915, the ideal forms that today make a Modigliani instantly recognizable emerged. They became firmly established when he started portraying the ordinary people who lived around him, in his buildings and his neighborhoods, people whose commonplace occupations and names have given birth to many remarkable pictures: *La Belle Epicière* and *The Servant* (1916), *La Fioraia (The Blooming Flower)*, *Popolana (The Common Artist)*, *The Little Farmer*, *La Rousse au Pendentif* (1918), *The Young Milkmaid*, *La Bohemienne*, *Gypsy Woman with Baby*, *The Young Apprentice*, and *Little Boy in Blue Jacket* (1919).

During these same years, Modigliani convinced several acquaintances to sit for him, including Lucienne Raymonde, Adrienne Elvire, and Marie—resulting in memorable portraits. These supposedly "cajoled" sittings reached a pinnacle of elegance and power in the portraits he painted of Hanka Zborowski and, in 1919, of Lunia Czechowska, as *Woman with Fan*.

Although Modigliani did paint several men, it is the women Modigliani painted with whom his art reached the highest perfection. His female models, with their softer contours, enabled Modigliani to strive for an idealized plasticity of form. He was able to elongate their bodies and faces to create exquisite new combinations of curves and lines; he was able to better see the expressive potential within the human form and bring it to light, pure and true, without any type of mannerism or pretension. In short, the female body inspired him. It succeeded in fully satisfying his innate yearnings for elegant forms and harmonious arabesques. Nowhere is this more evident than in the absolute masterpieces Modigliani painted of his lover, Jeanne Hébuterne, especially in the series of nudes he painted in 1917 and 1918.

The last portrait of Jeanne Hébuterne (1920) is considered the most classical of all of Modigliani's paintings, with influences that date back to the Sienese Virgin in Simone Martini's fourteenth-century *Annunciation*. In Modigliani's creation, the Virgin as Jeanne is easily recognizable. The figure is precisely the same as in the original, but its form is reversed.

In this and other portraits of Jeanne, Modigliani shows the strong link he still had to the great traditions of his native country. His expressions of femininity achieve the highest degree of tenderness, but at the same time they have an unsettling quality, which is the same subtle tension that characterized the Italian great masters.

Modigliani's *Self-Portrait*, painted in 1919, illuminates the qualities he had previously captured only in his portraits of Jeanne, his soulmate and great love. This painting, with its classical underpinnings, turns his melancholy stance into that of a handsome but severely aloof angel.

Modigliani's last three paintings were also portraits. The first two show his friends, the young Baranowski and Survage. He and Jeanne lived at their home in Nice during the winter of 1918-1919. Jeanne gave birth to their daughter, Jeanne, during that time.

Modigliani's last portrait was entitled *Mario*. It is a drawing of a Greek musician completed the day before Modigliani's final illness.

A Too Brief Life

Modigliani's intense flame could not last. His passionate and turbulent life, torn with dramatic conflict between his weaknesses and his ideals, abruptly came to an end on January 25, 1920, at the Charite Hospital in Rue des Saints-Peres. He died of tuberculosis, but, before he breathed his last, he whispered, "Cara, cara Italia."

Jeanne was at his side, pregnant with their second child. She could not contain her grief. Her parents took her home and brought her to the bedroom that was once hers. While she lay in bed, sobbing, numb, and in shock, her parents discussed her in the next room. They were afraid of the scandal Jeanne would create if she lived at home. Here she was, unmarried, with a young daughter and another child on the way. They planned to give her some money, then send her away.

But that night, while everyone slept, Jeanne jumped from her bedroom window. She is buried alongside her beloved Amedeo in the cemetery of Père Lachaise.

Jeanne's legacy is bound forever with Modigliani. And Amedeo Modigliani's legacy is, of course, his great works of art. The purity of his painting, the classic strength of his sculpture, and his troubled, romantic life make him a unique figure in the panorama of modern art—a great master who refused to assimilate into the artistic currents that surrounded him.

But Modigliani's greatness came from more than a stubborn genius. Despite the illness, addiction, and material difficulties that continued until the day he died, he created a perfect and complete body of work, from which nothing is absent, in which there is not a single trace of decline. His work provides the evidence: Modigliani's very last paintings are not only his most beautiful, but his most powerful as well.

"You are not alive unless you know you are living," Modigliani wrote on one of the walls of his studio. And he lives still, in the hearts and minds of everyone who gazes at his work and feels what is it like to be not only human, fragile and strong, but also very much alive.

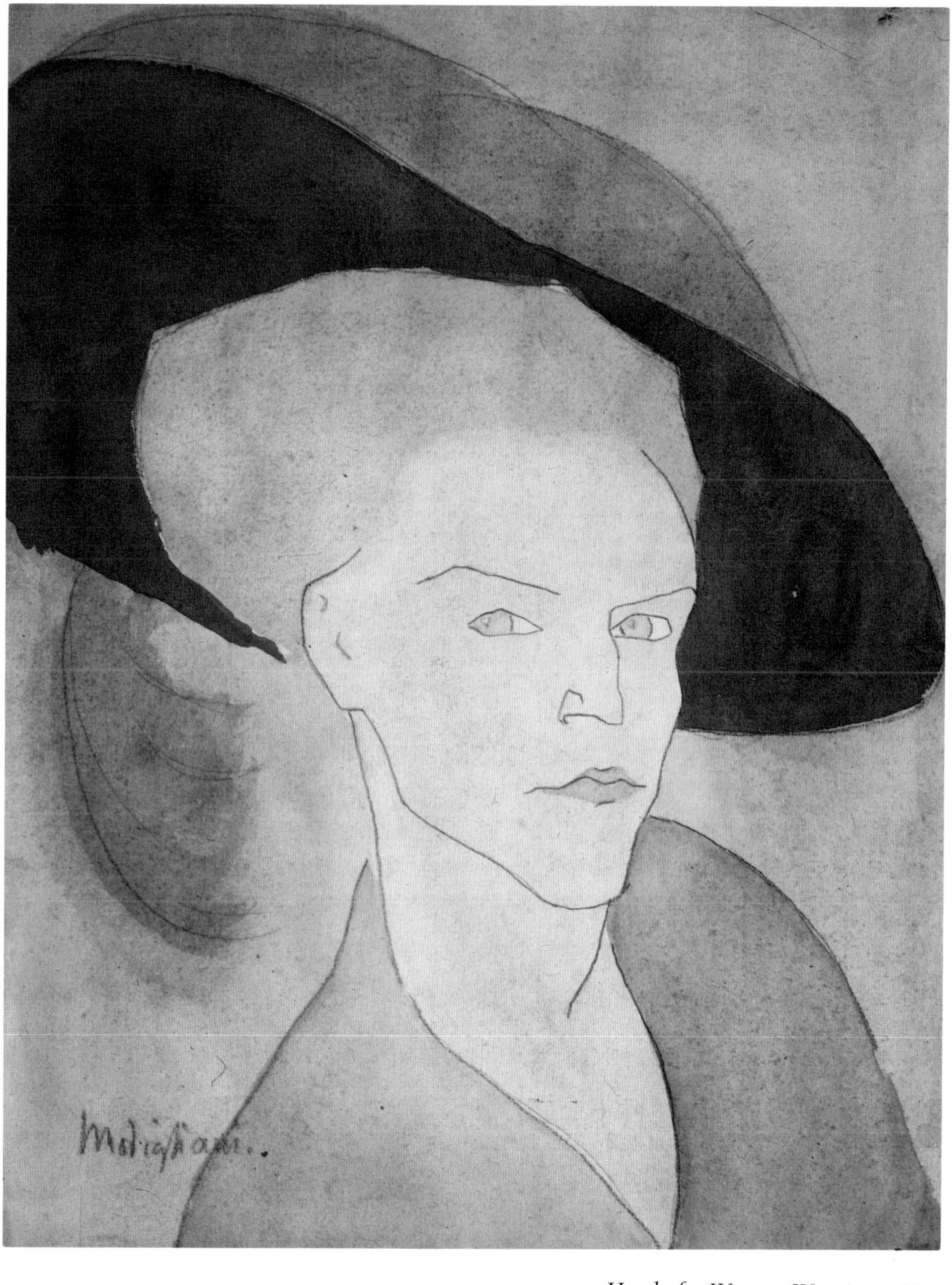

Head of a Woman Wearing a Hat

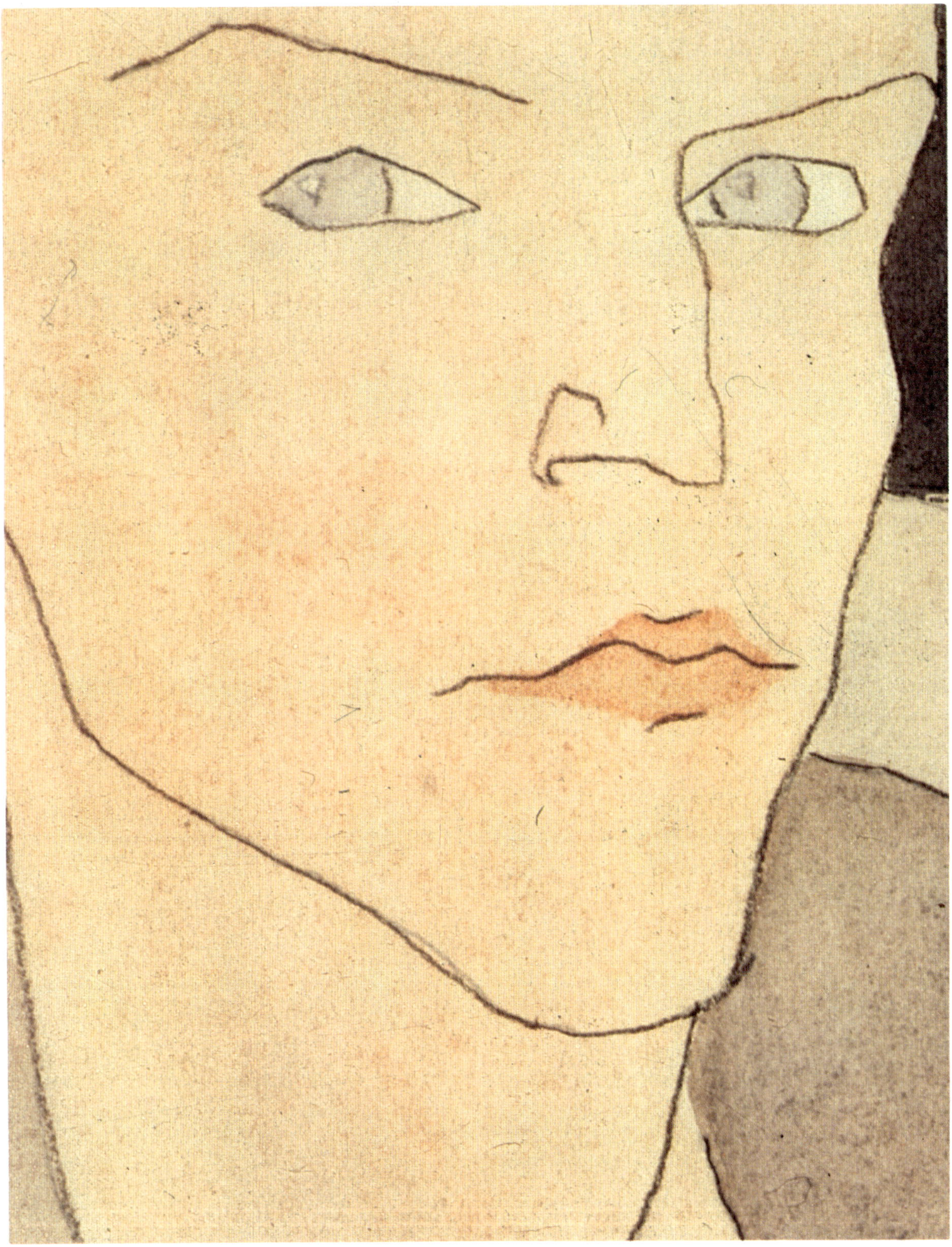

Head of a Woman Wearing a Hat (Detail)

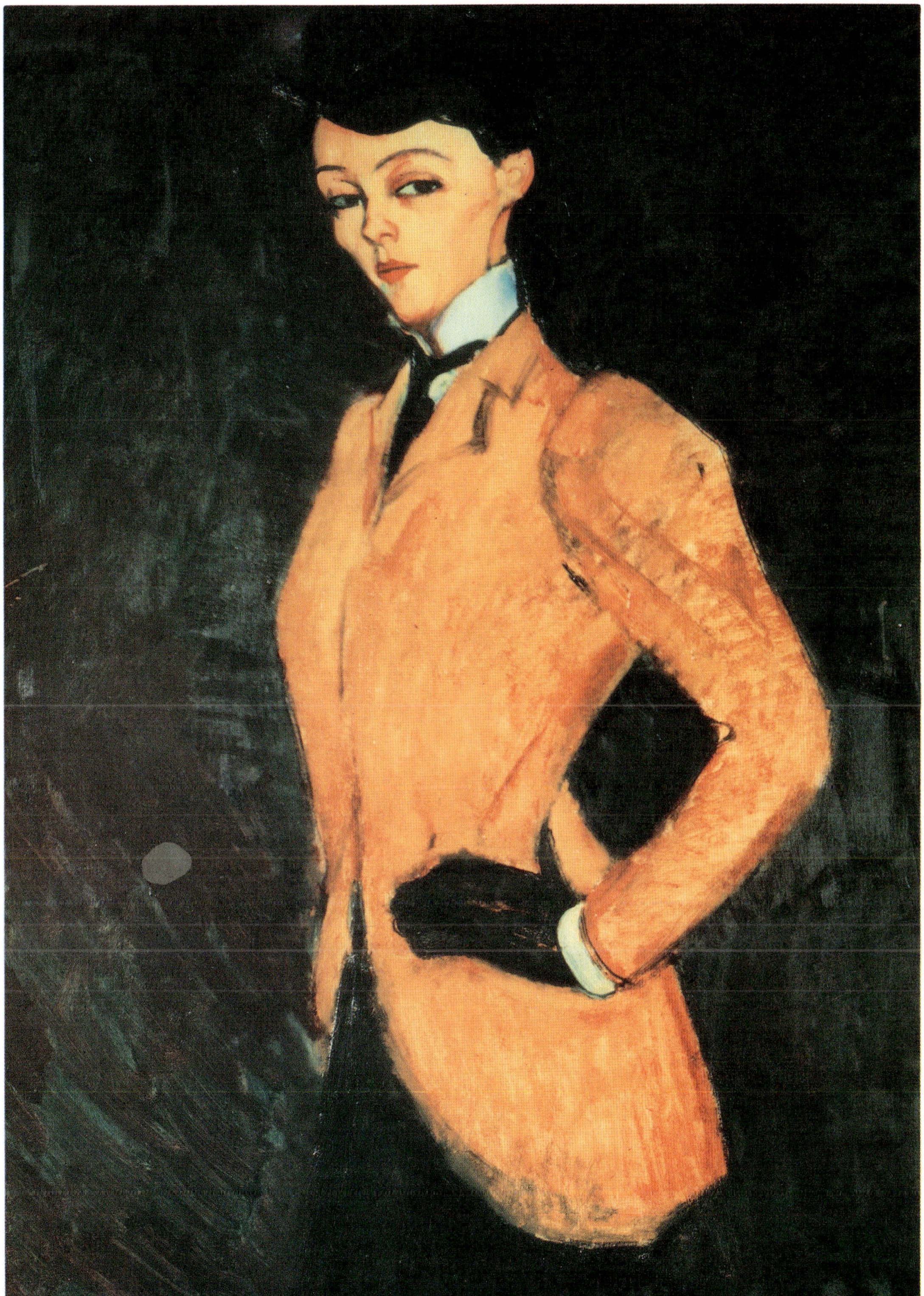

The Equestrienne (L'Amazone)

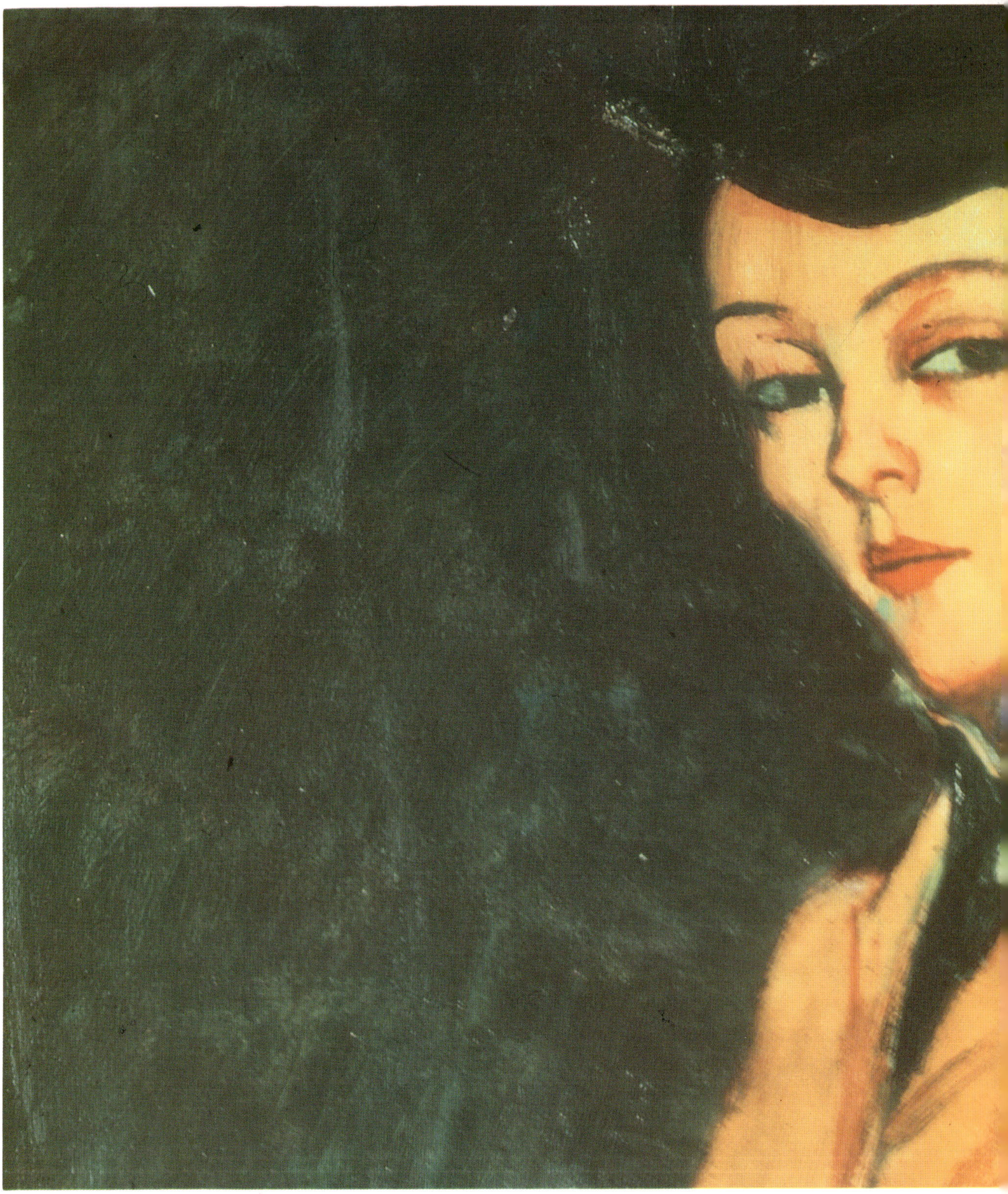

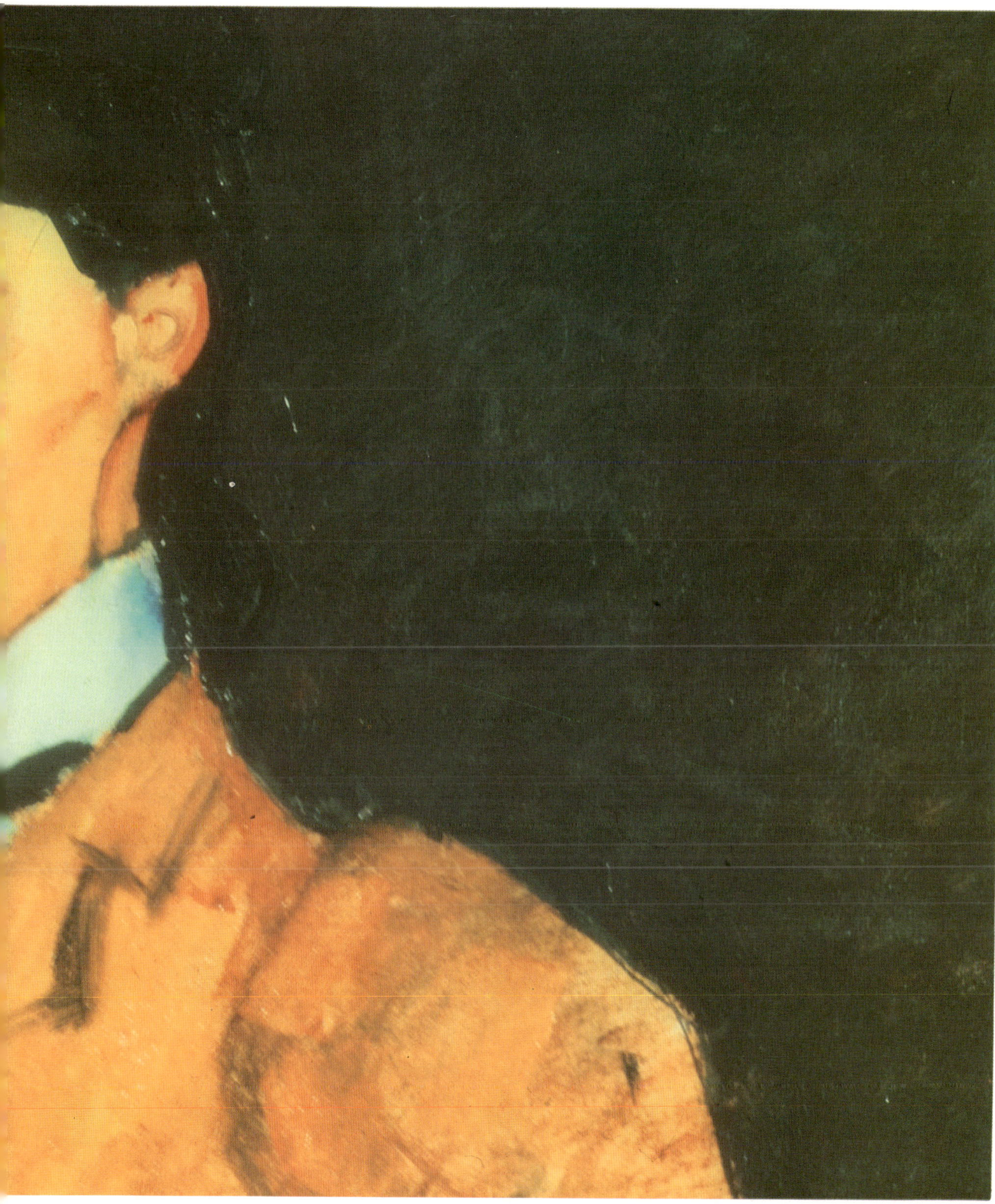

The Equestrienne (Detail)

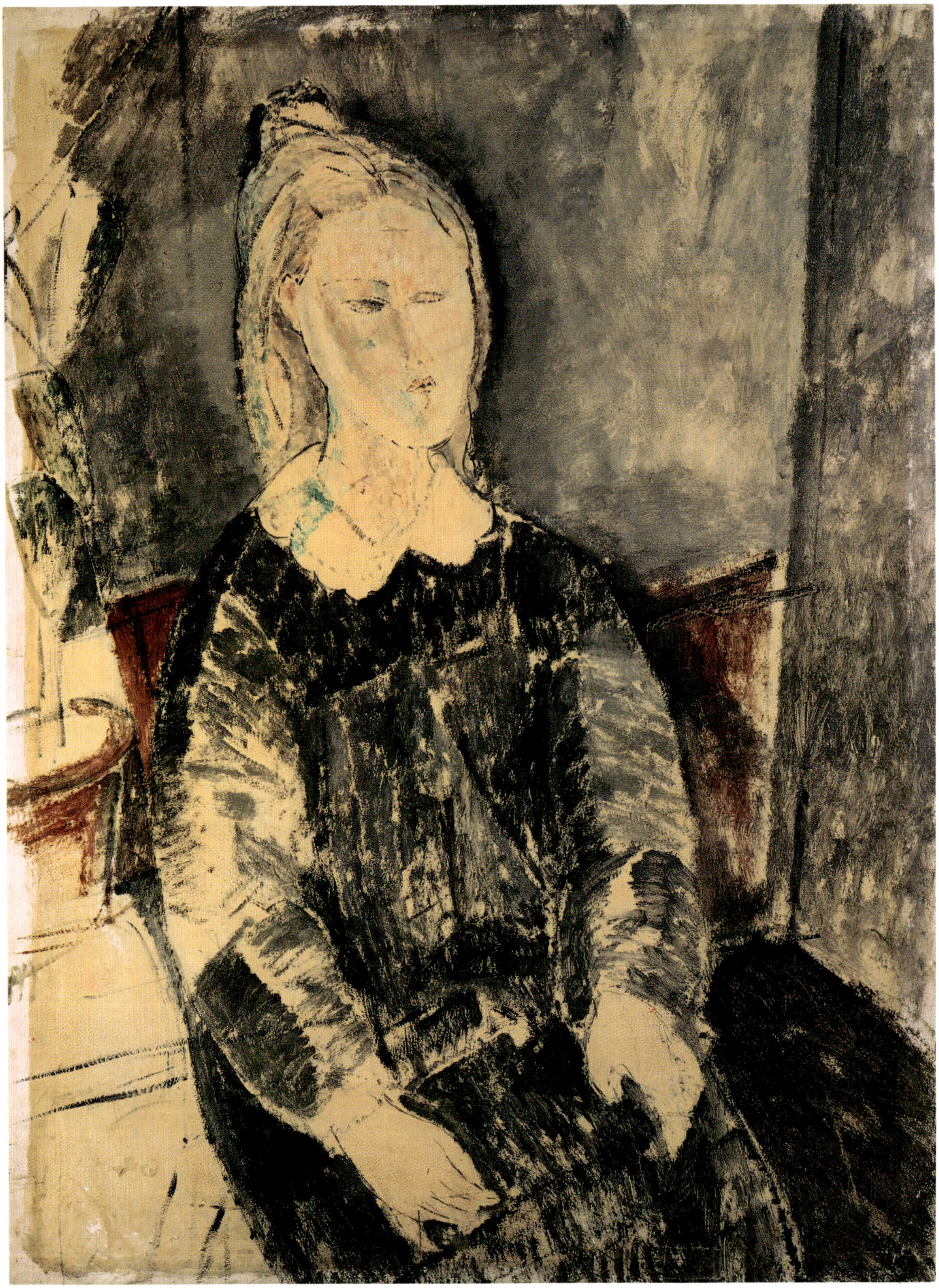

Woman in Blue

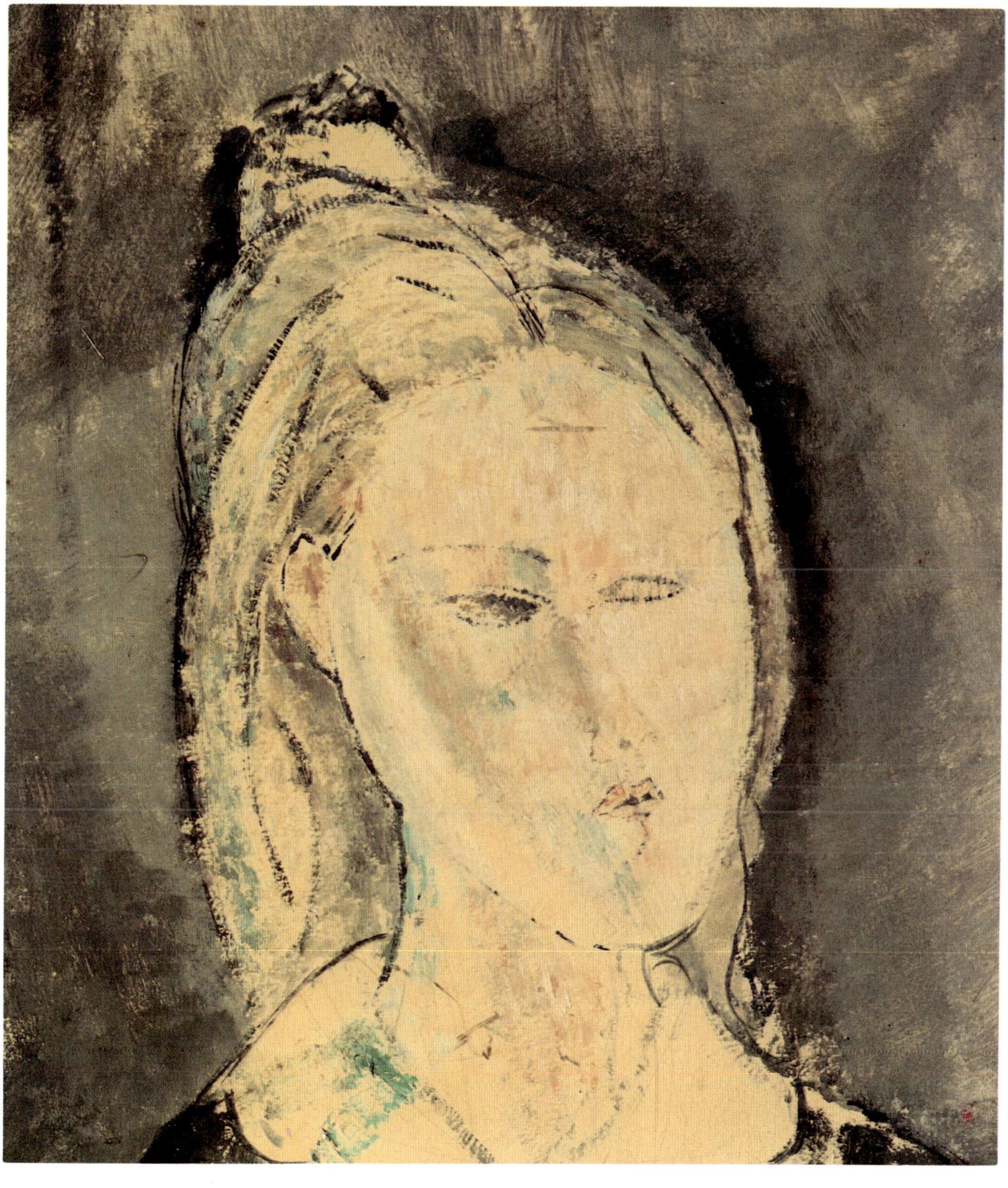

Woman in Blue (Detail)

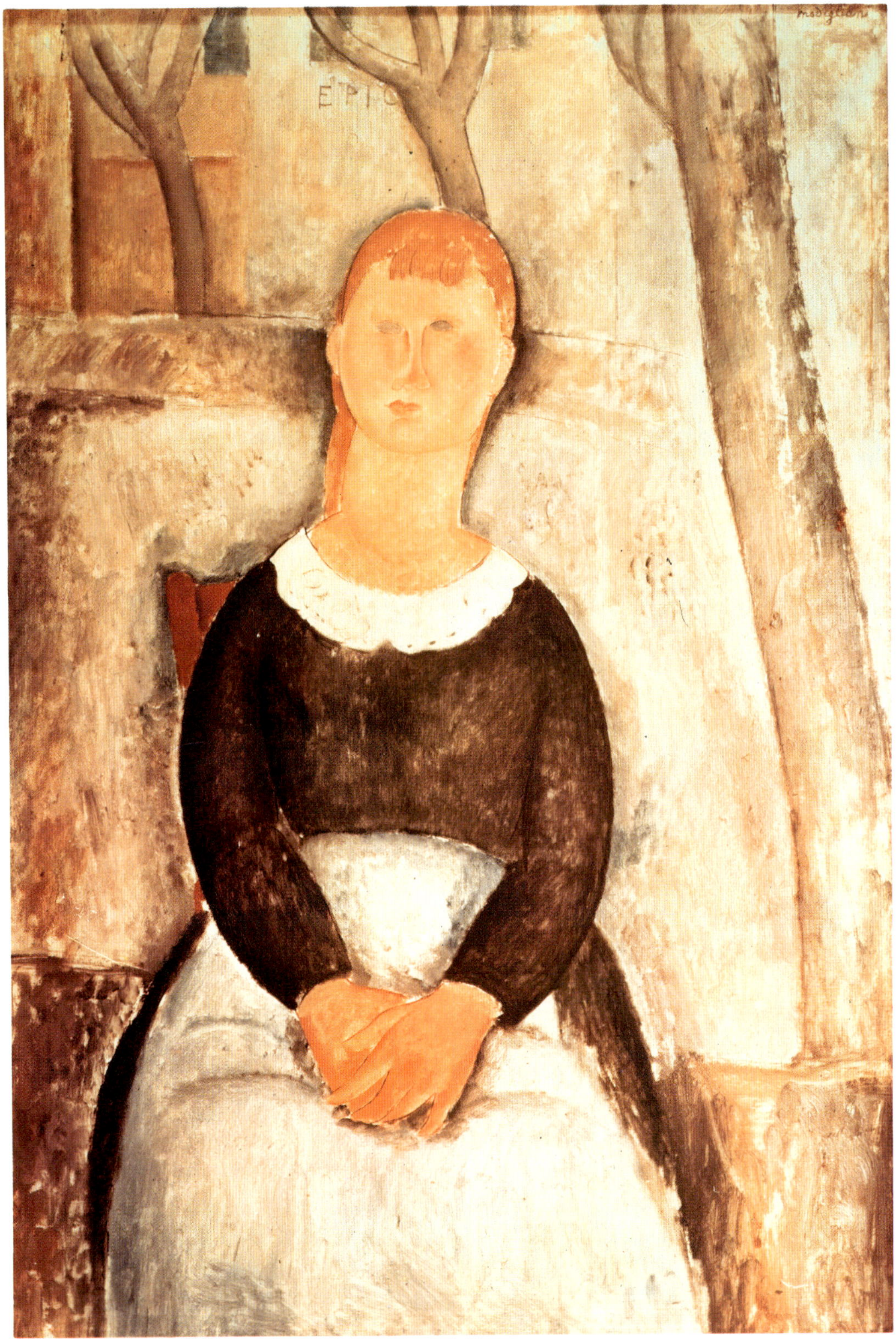

La Belle Epicière

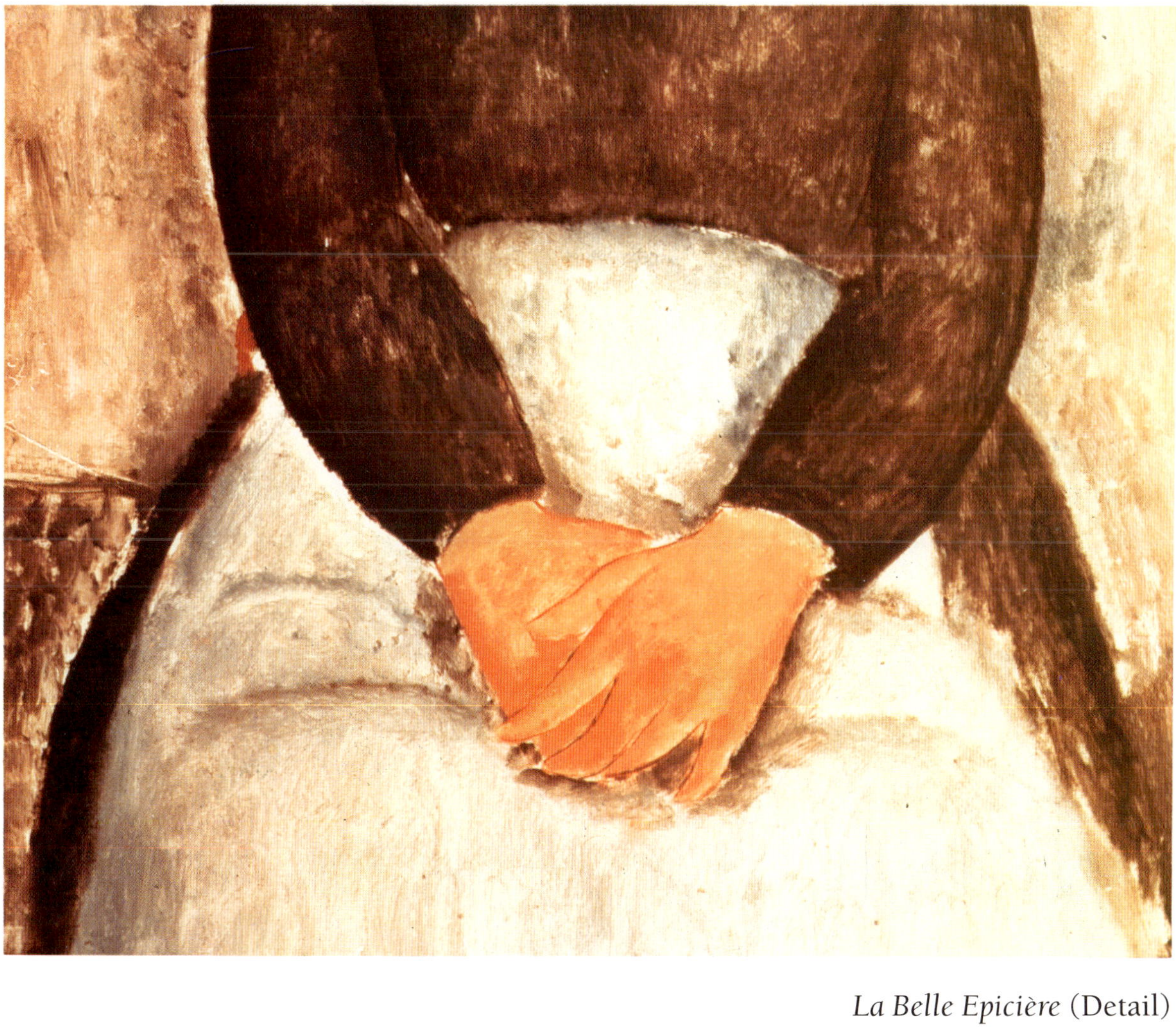

La Belle Epicière (Detail)

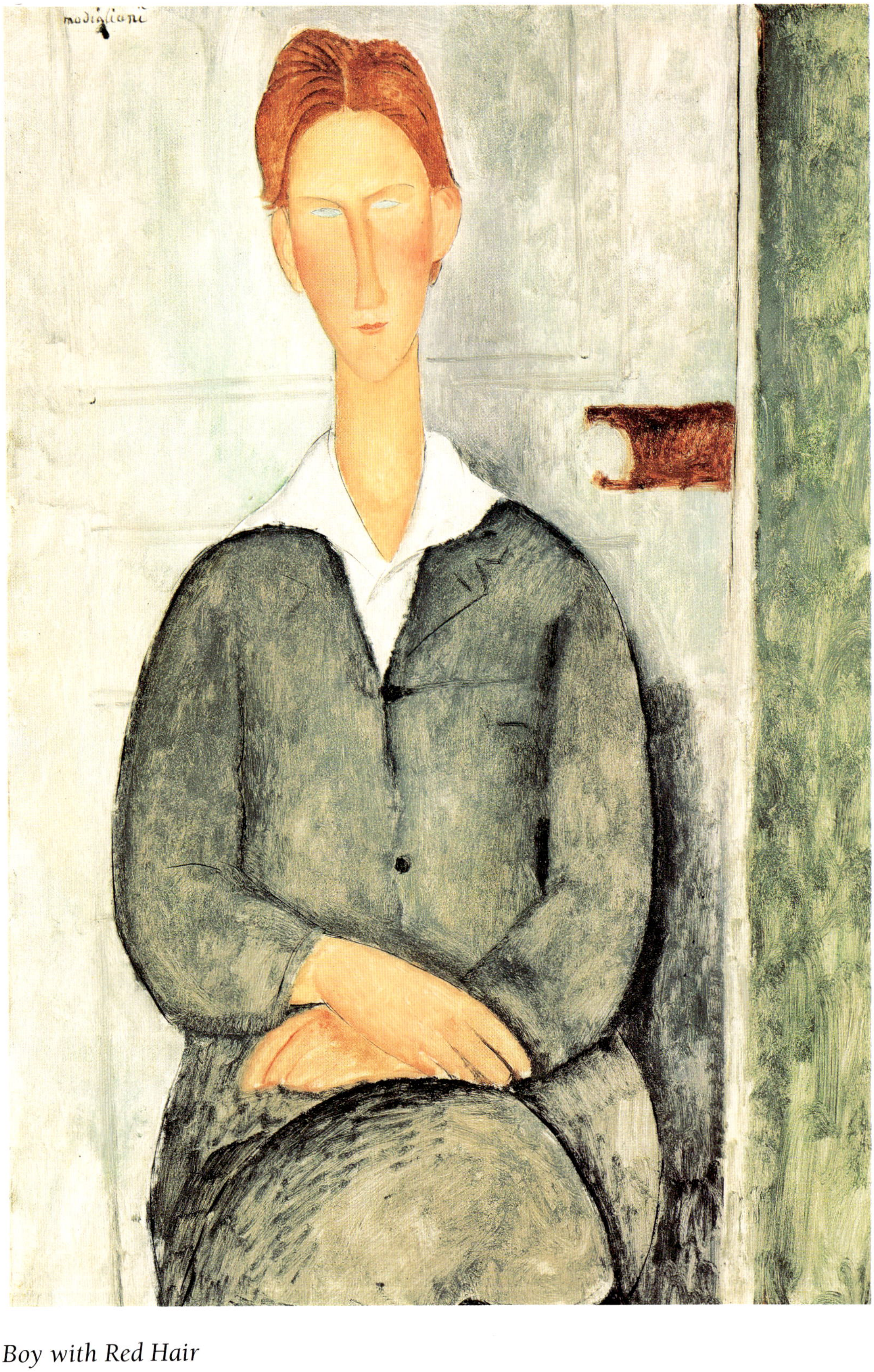

Boy with Red Hair

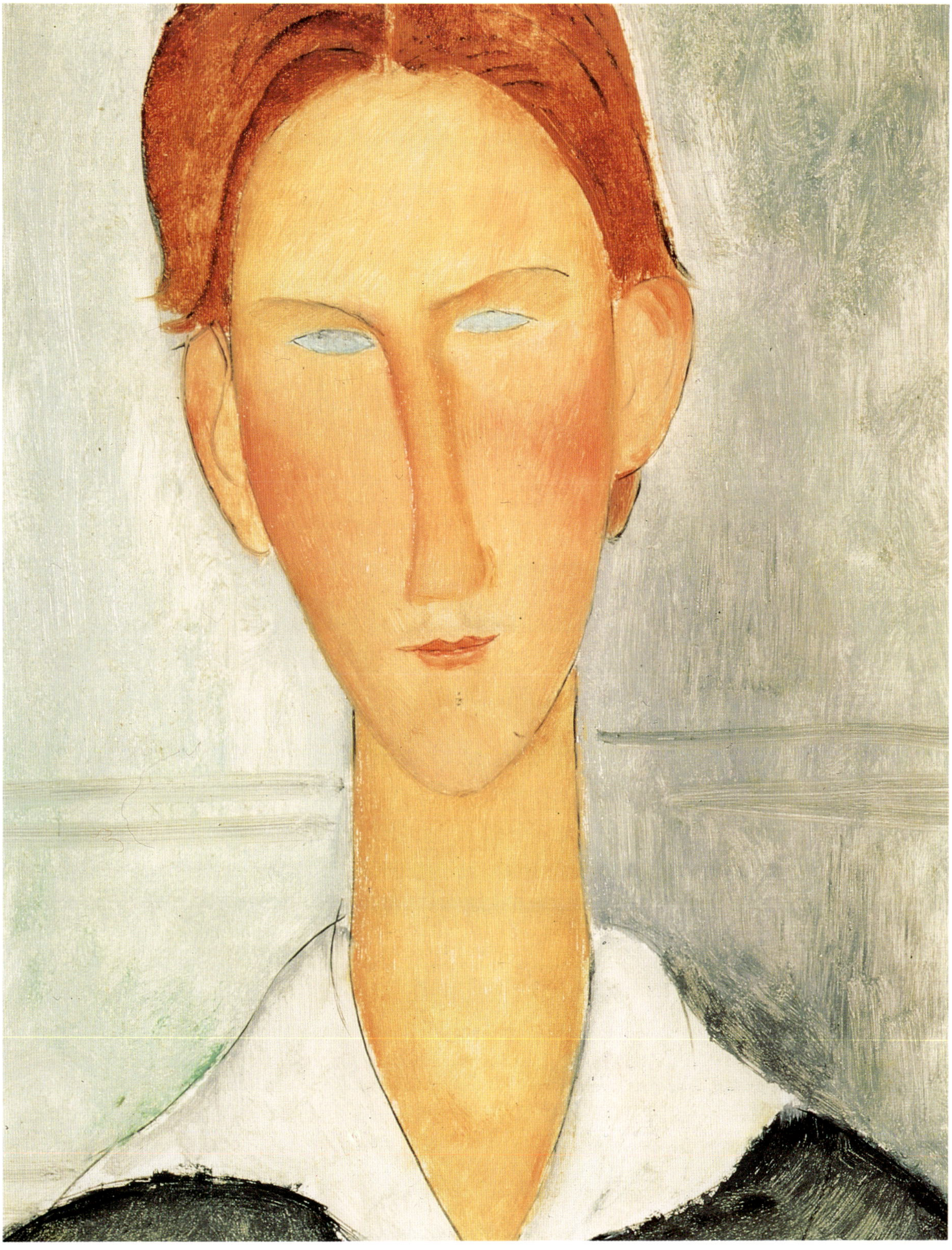

Boy with Red Hair (Detail)

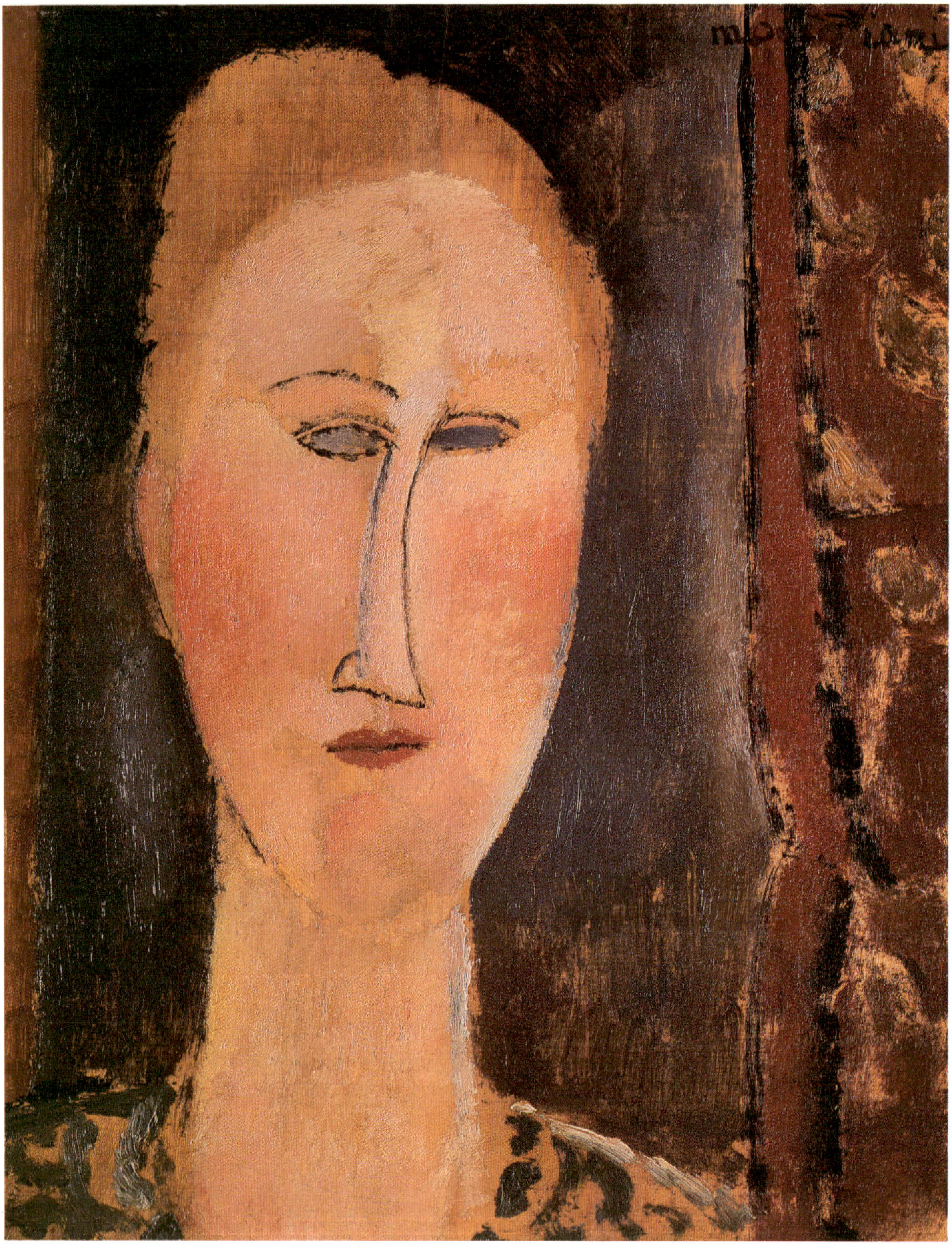

Head of a Woman

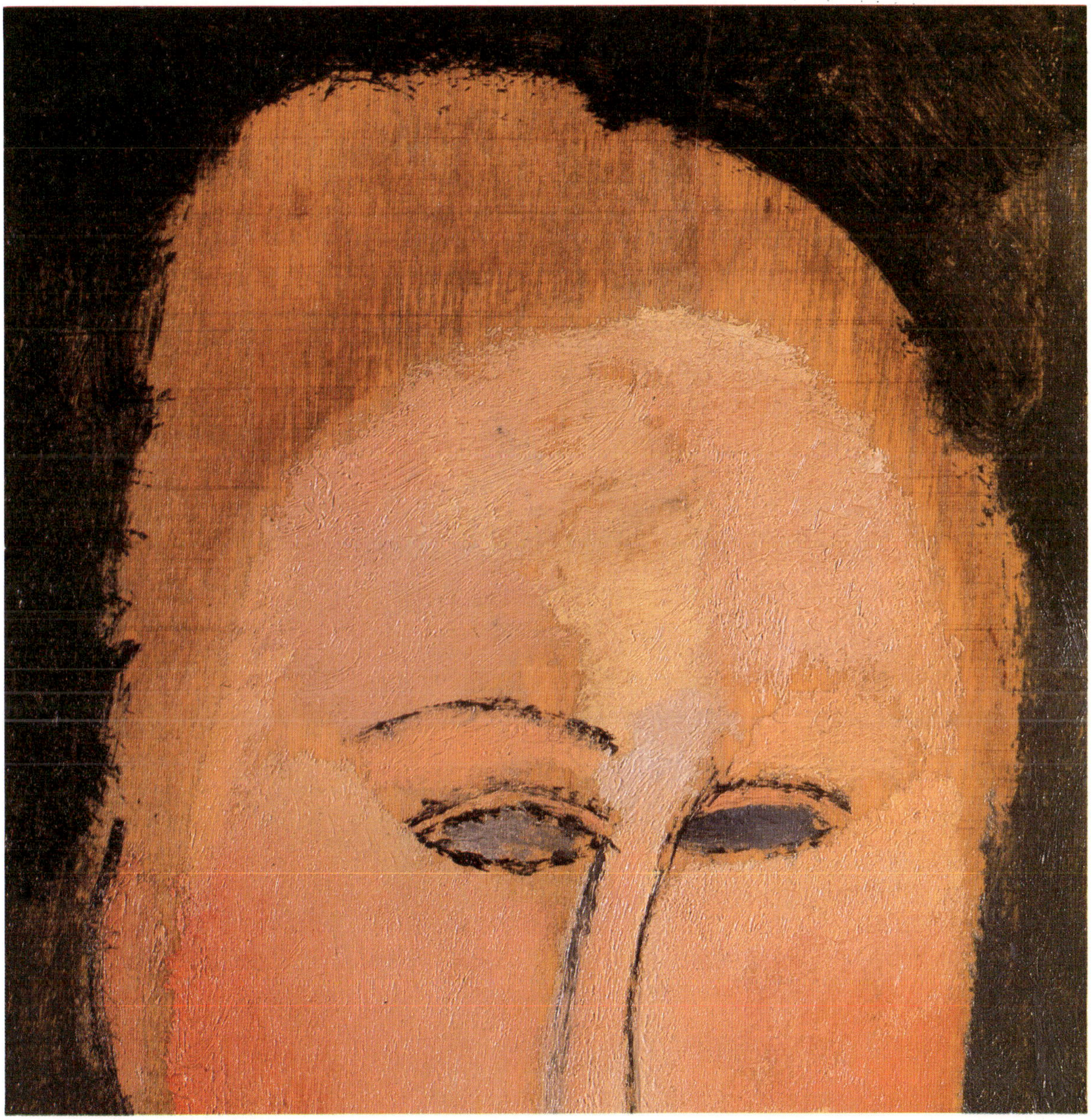

Head of a Woman (Detail)

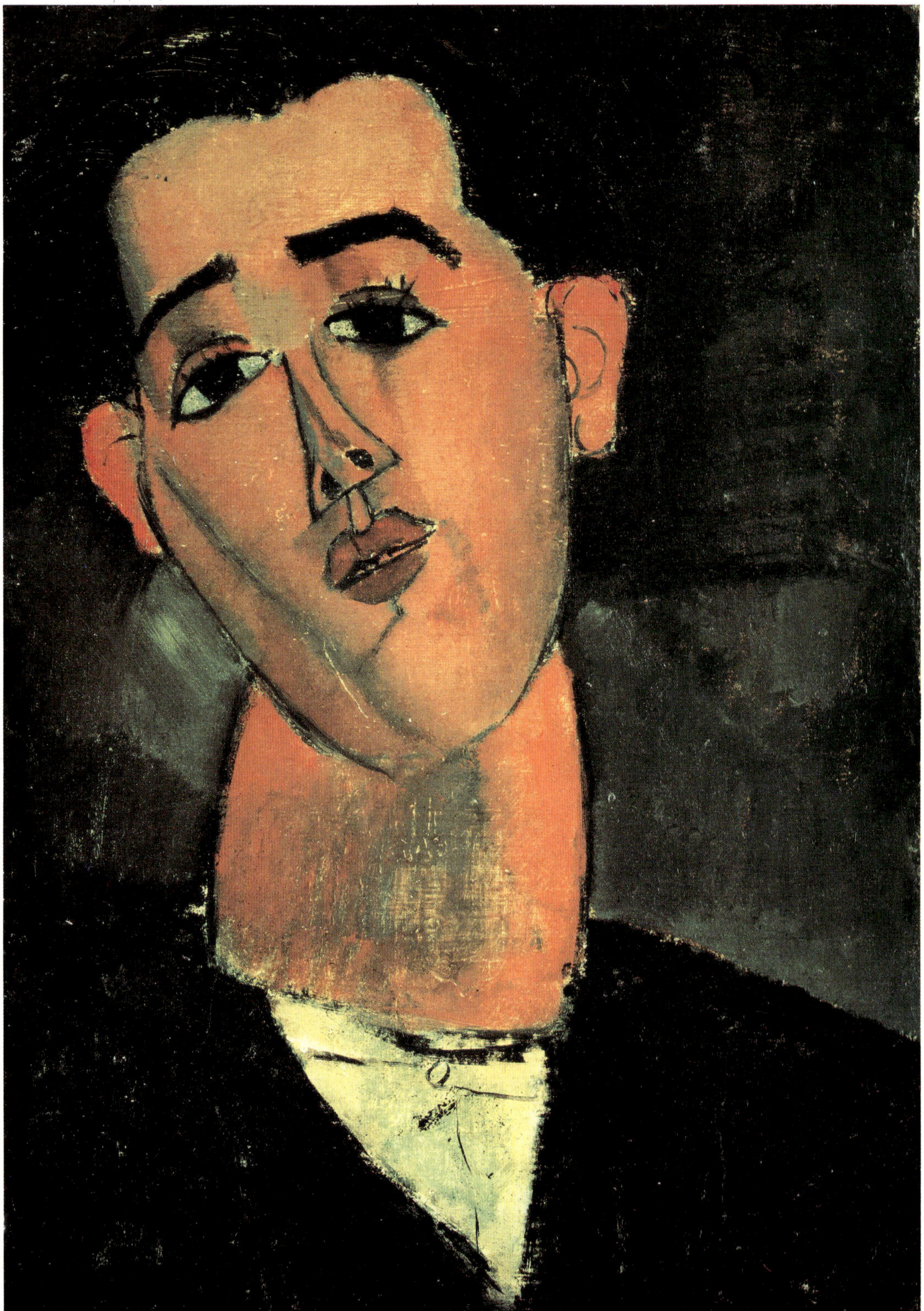

Juan Gris

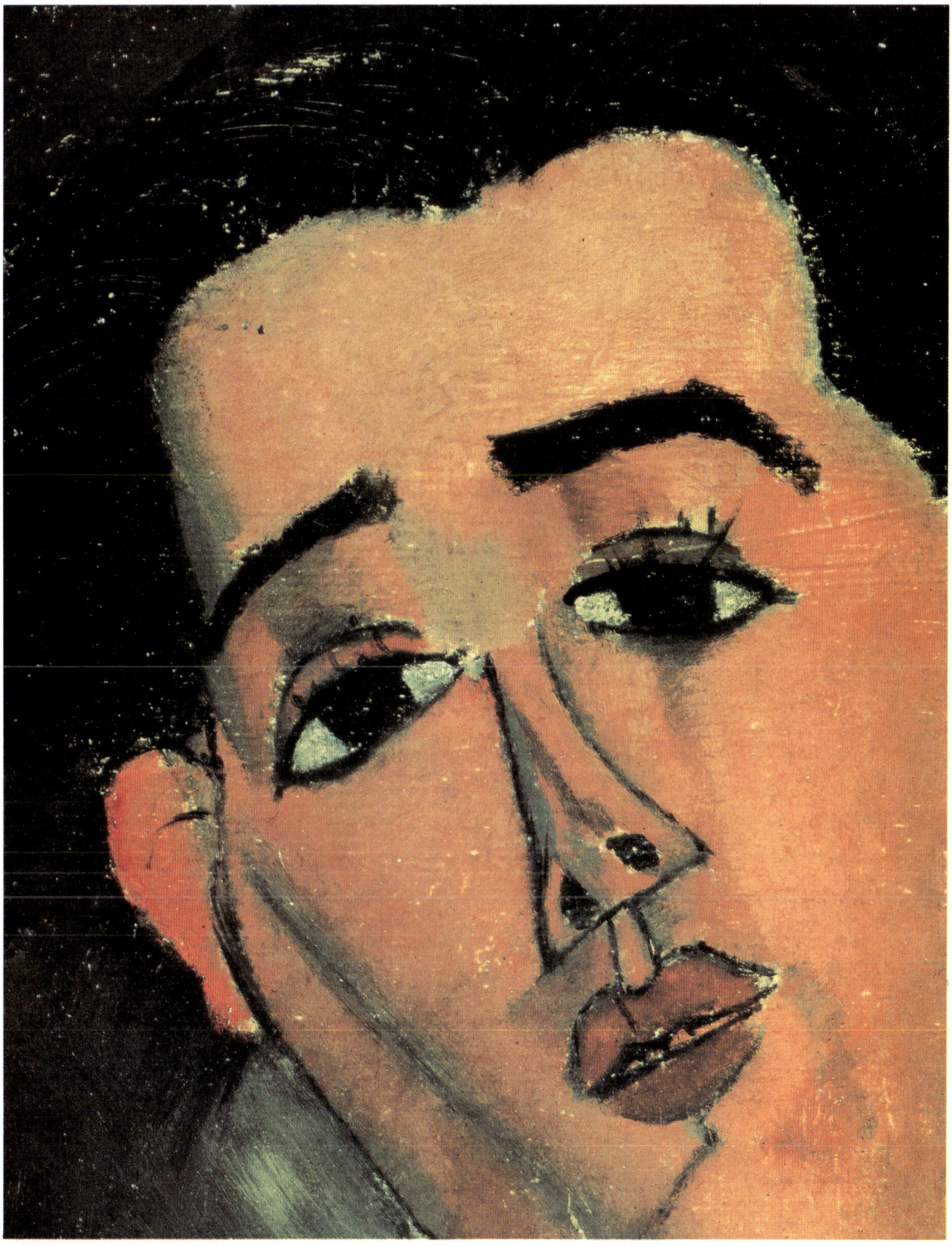

Juan Gris (Detail)

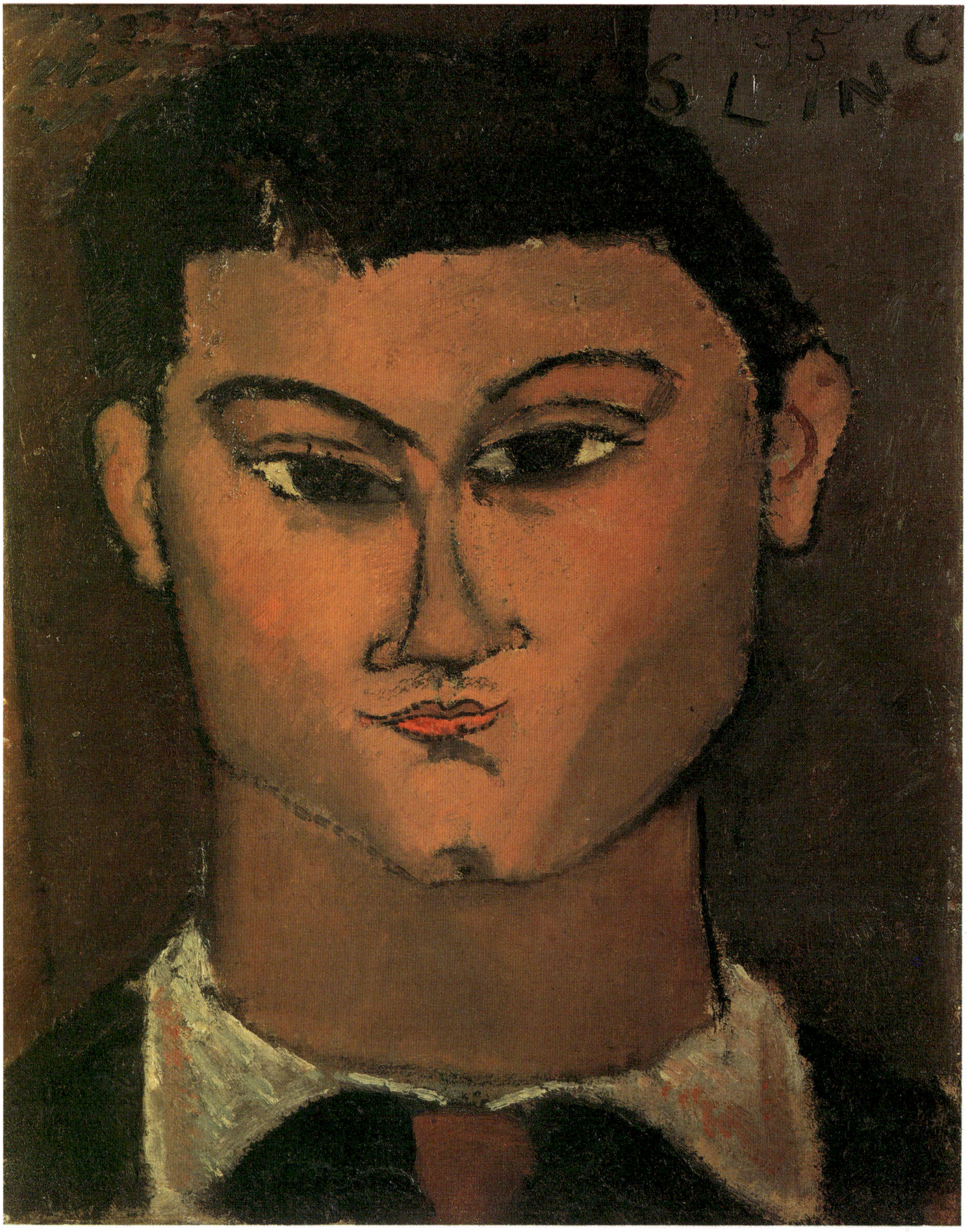

Head of Moïse Kisling (Detail)

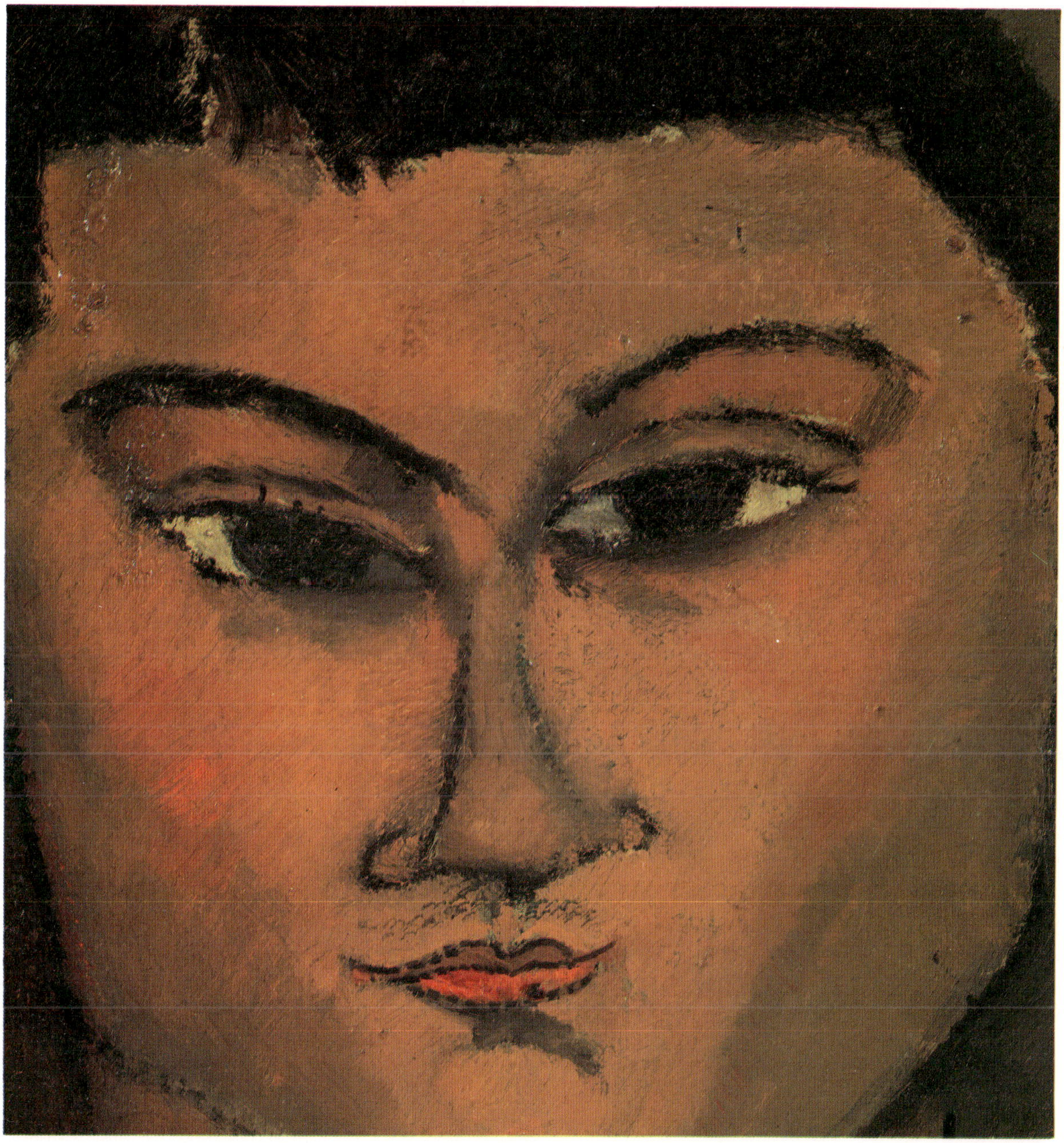

Head of Moïse Kisling

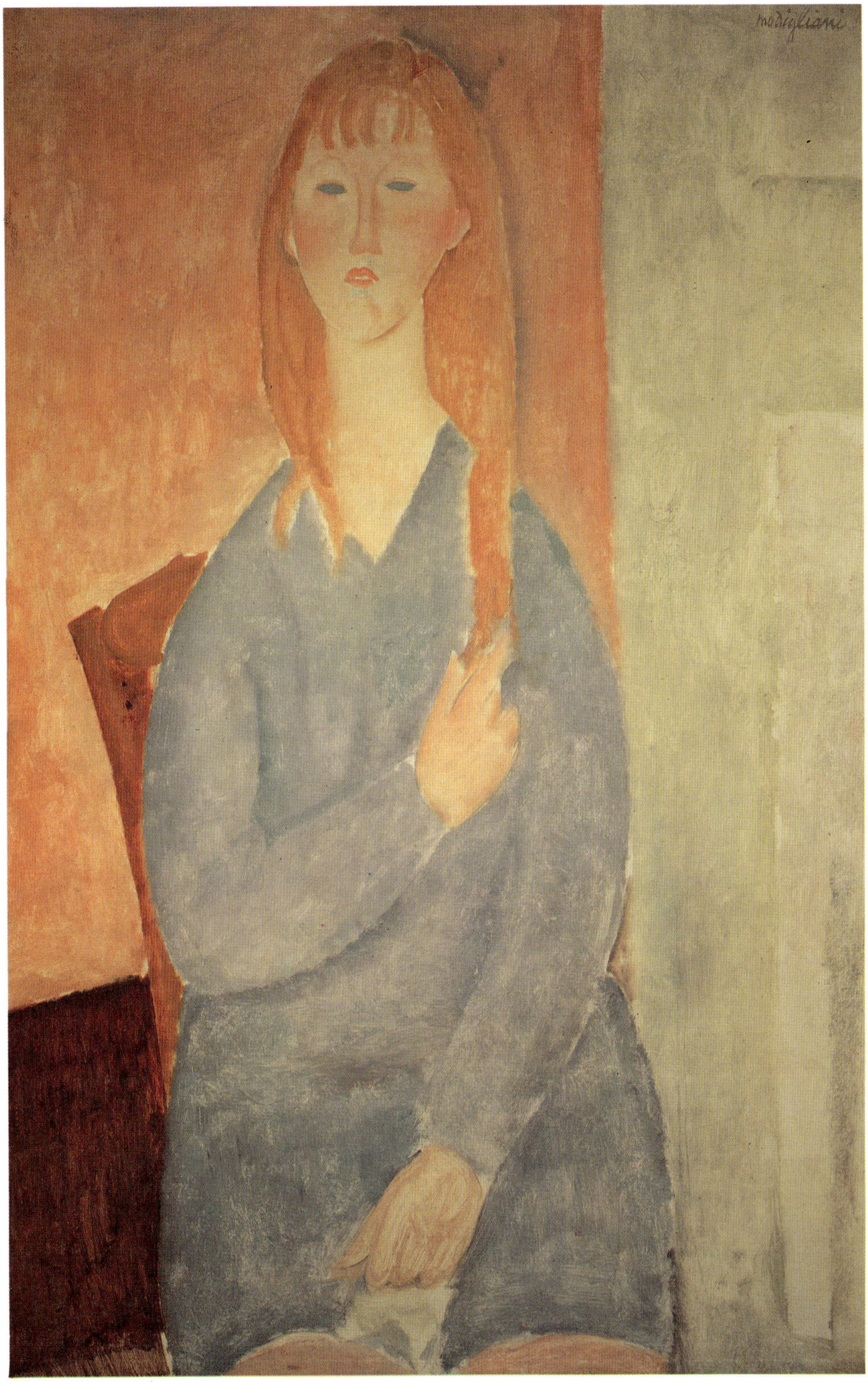

Girl in Blue Dress

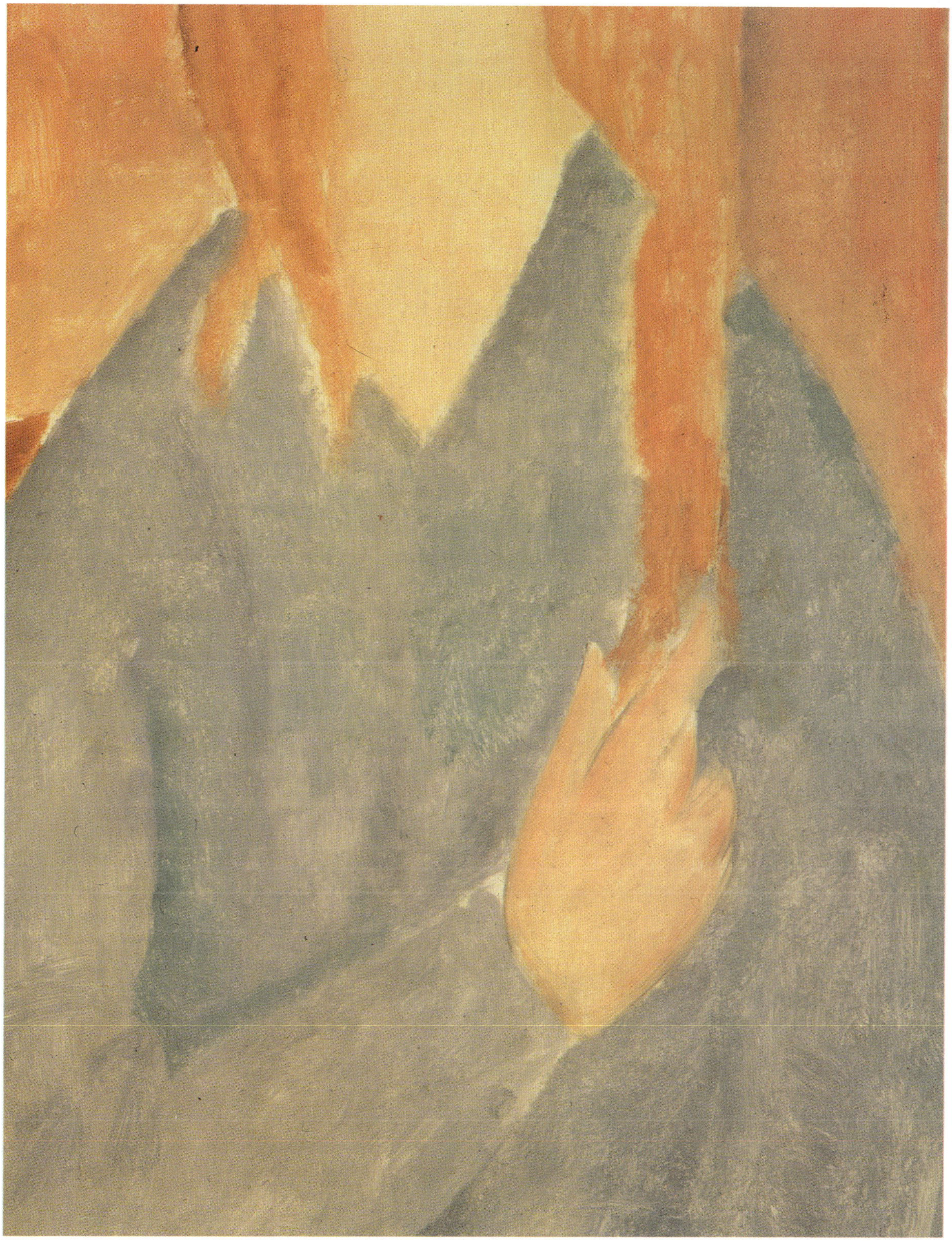

Girl in Blue Dress (Detail)

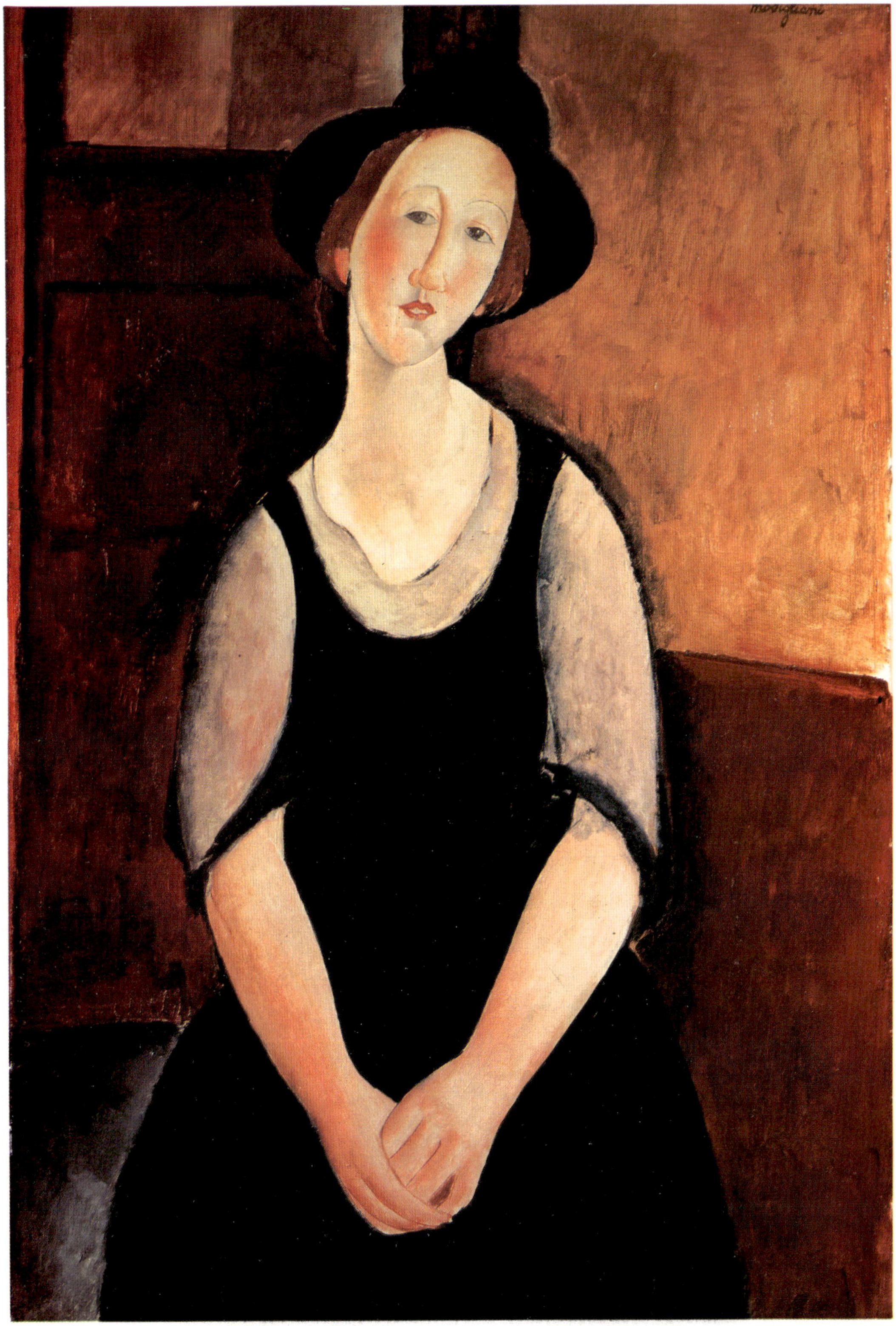

Portrait of Thora Klinchlowstrom

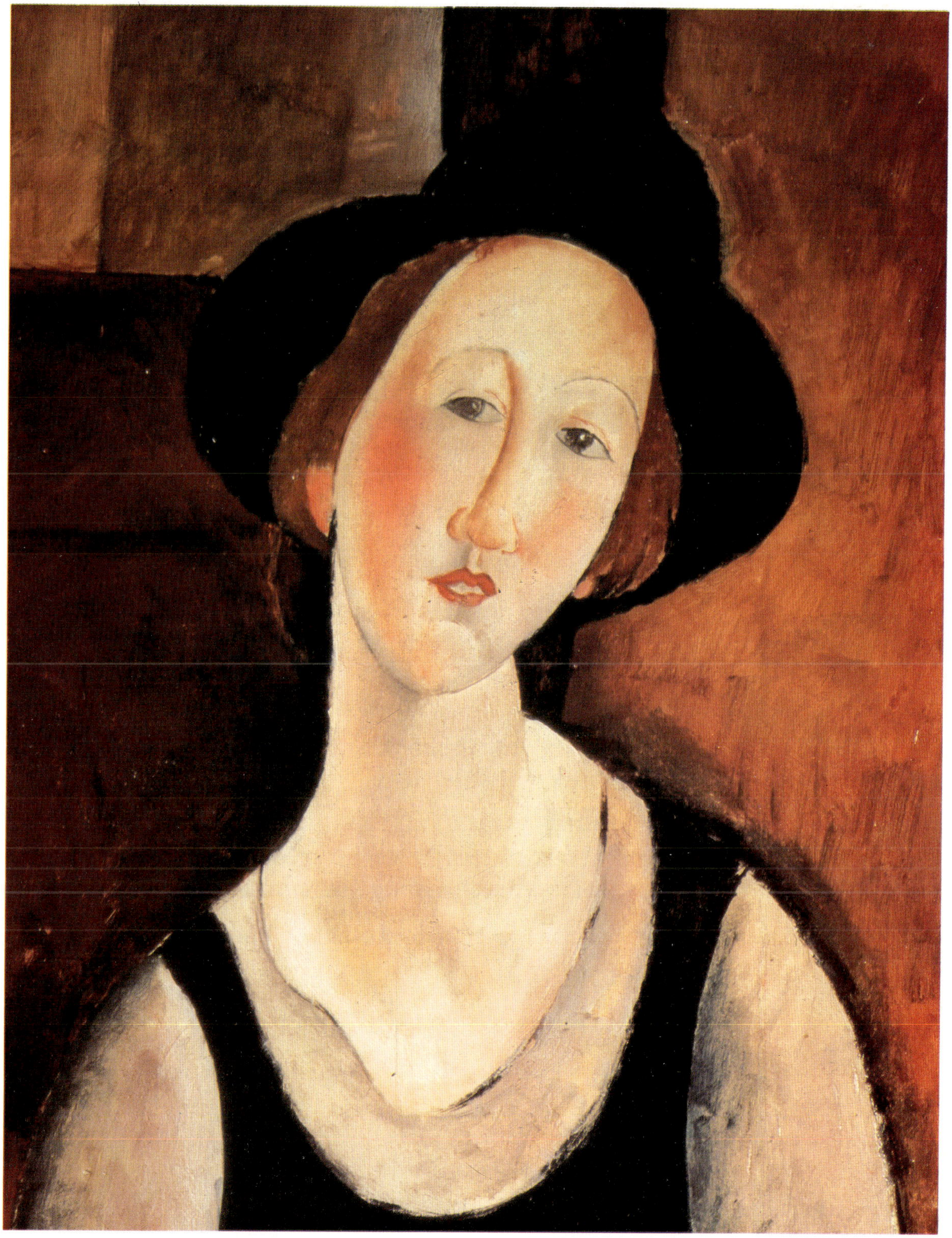

Portrait of Thora Klinchlowstrom (Detail)

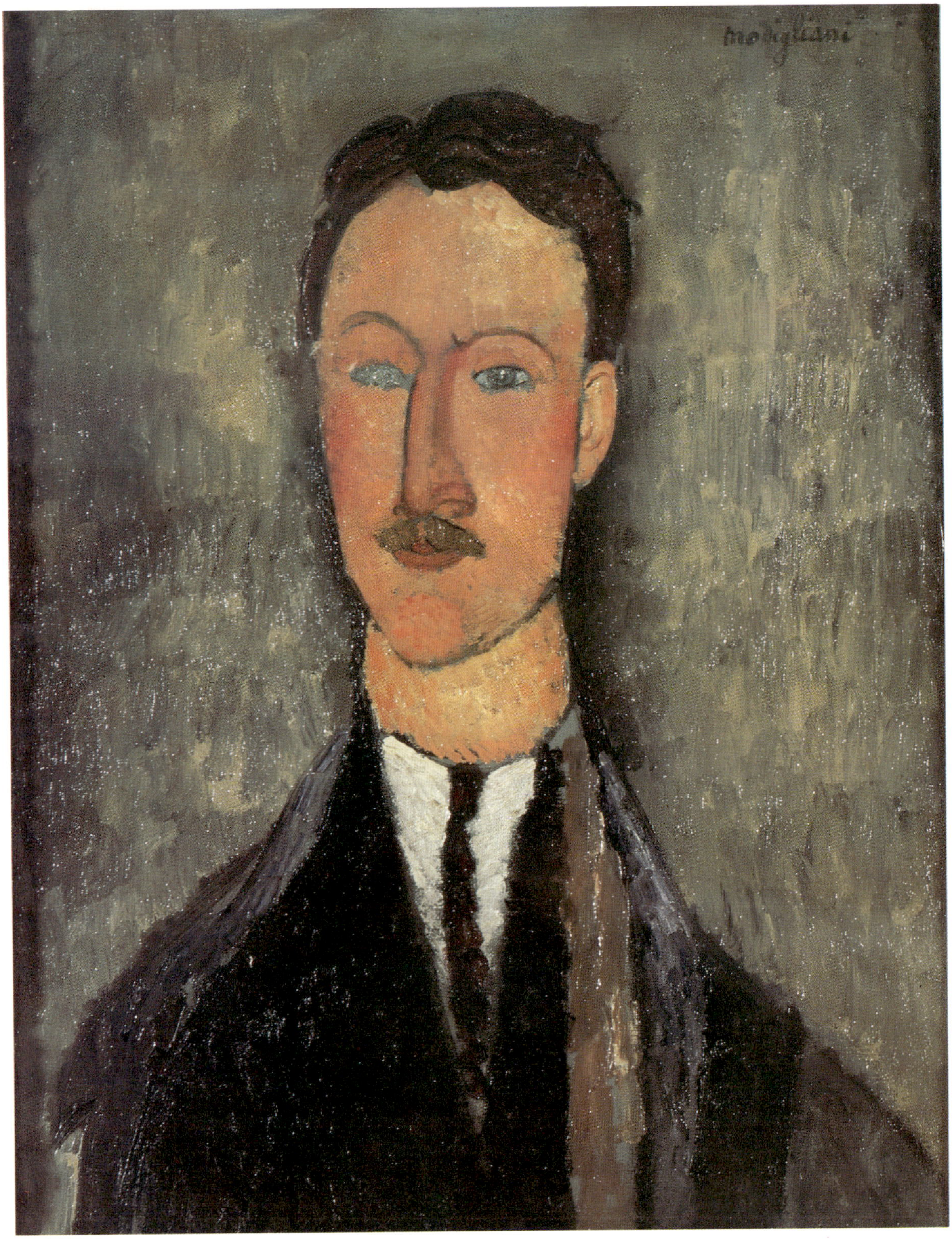

Léopold Survage

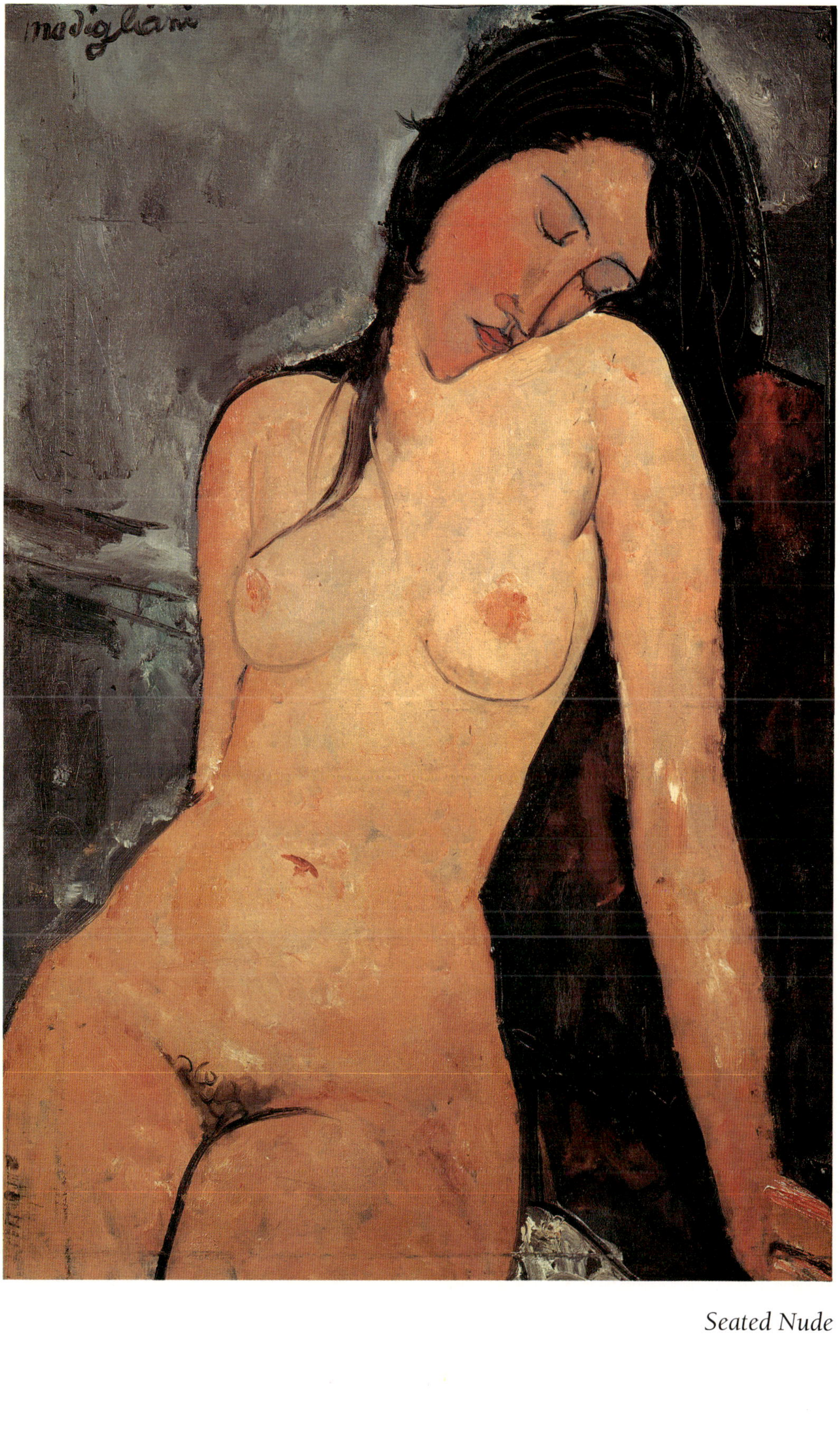

Seated Nude

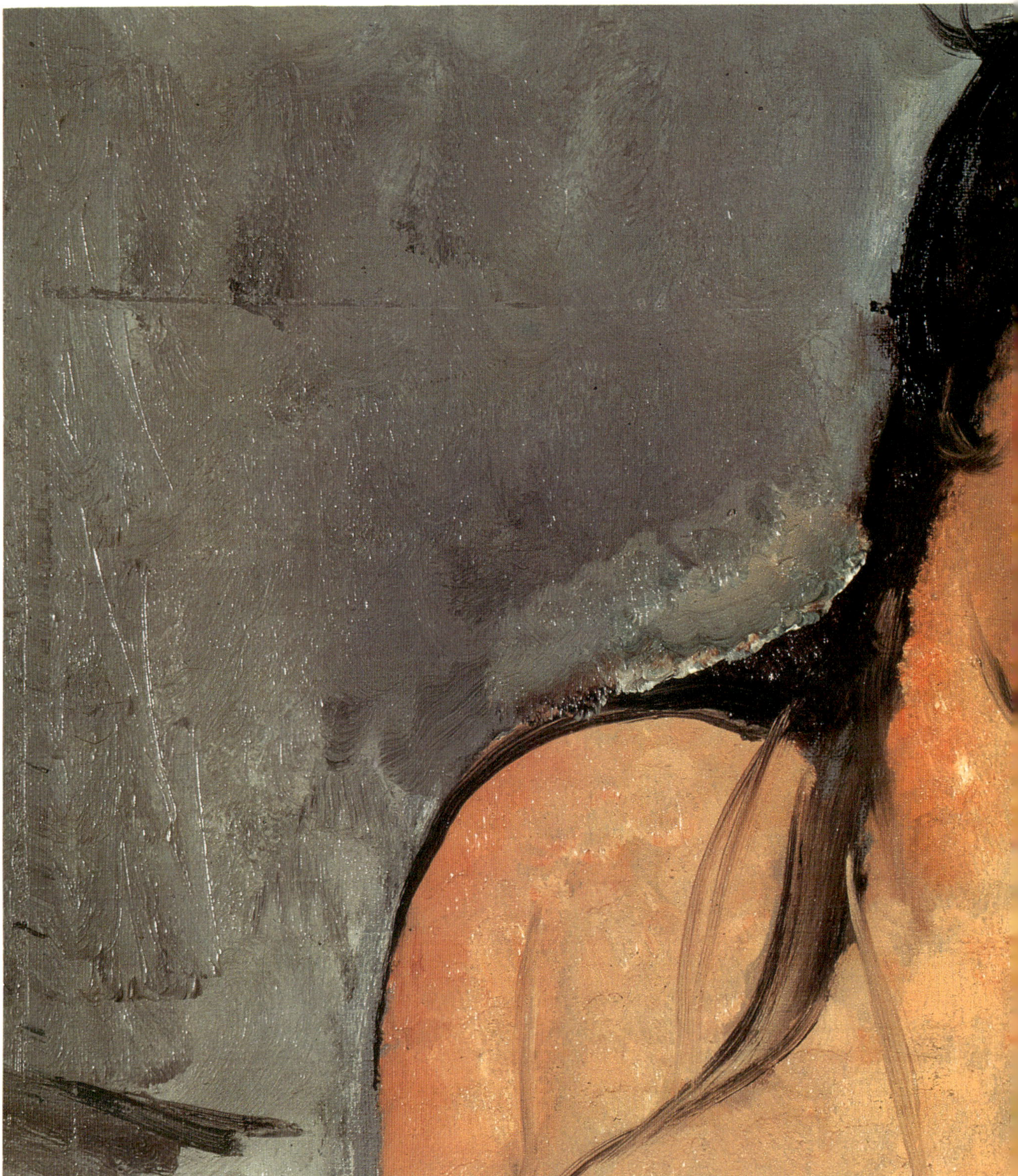

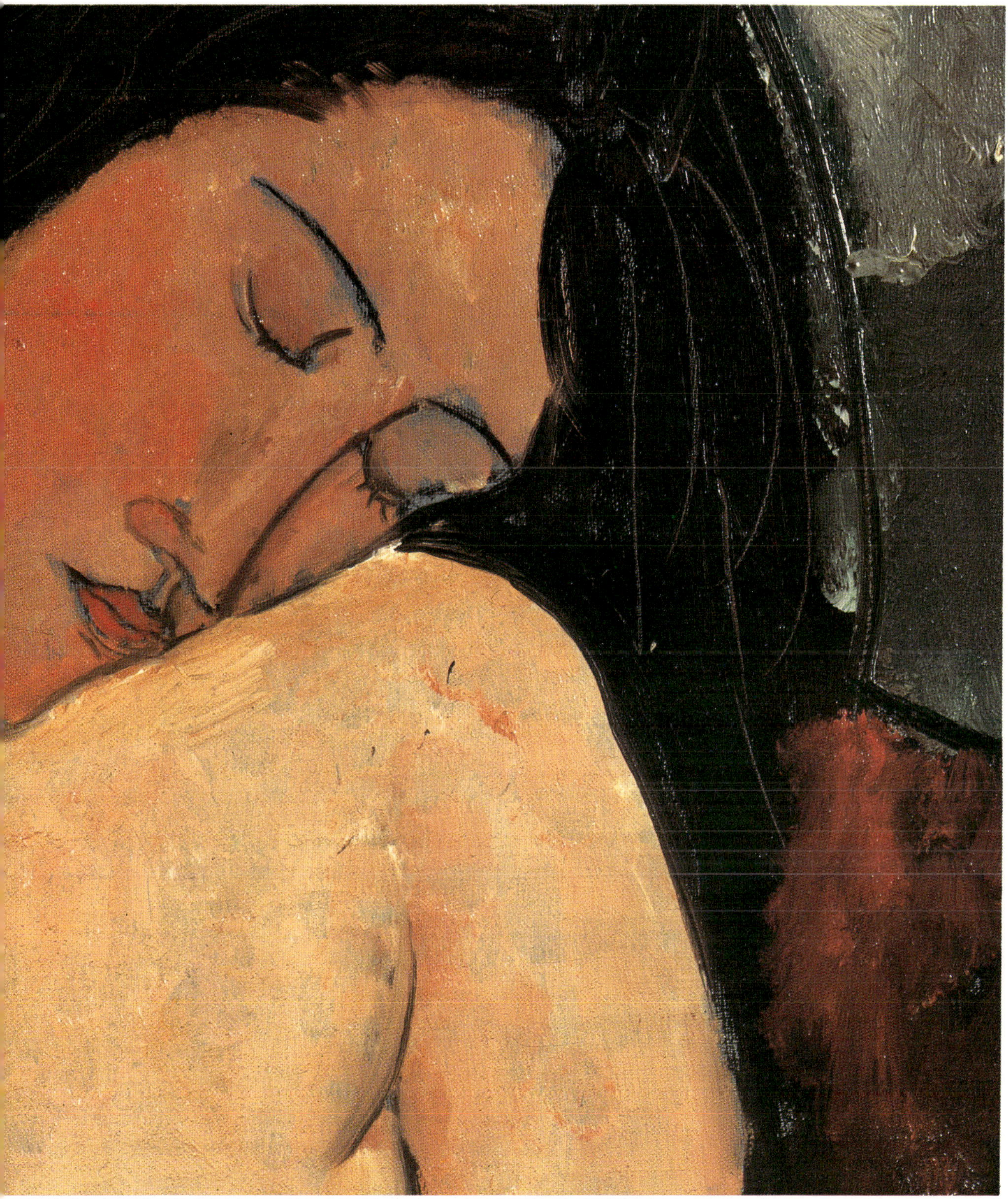

Seated Nude (Detail)

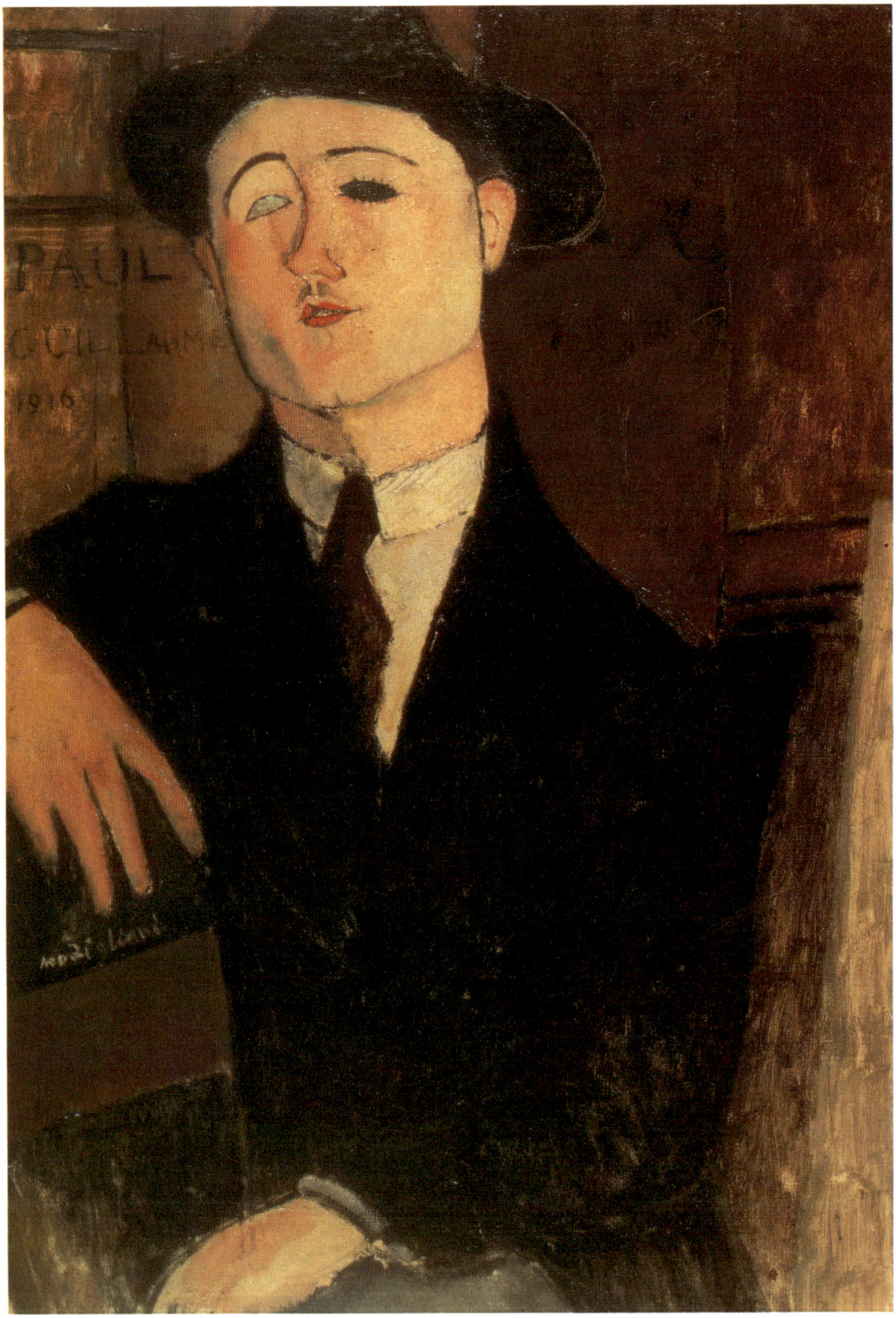

Portrait of Paul Guillaume

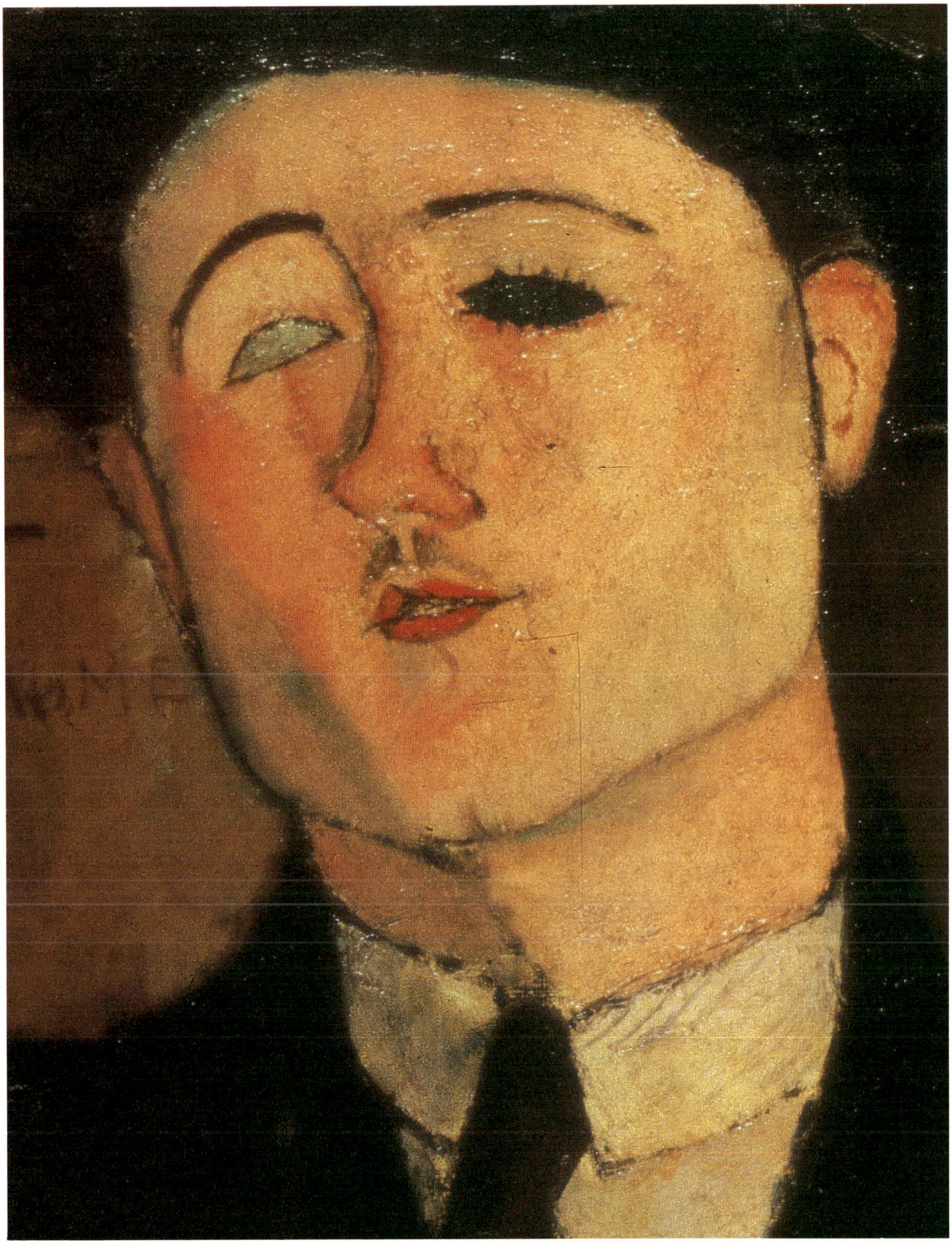

Portrait of Paul Guillaume (Detail)

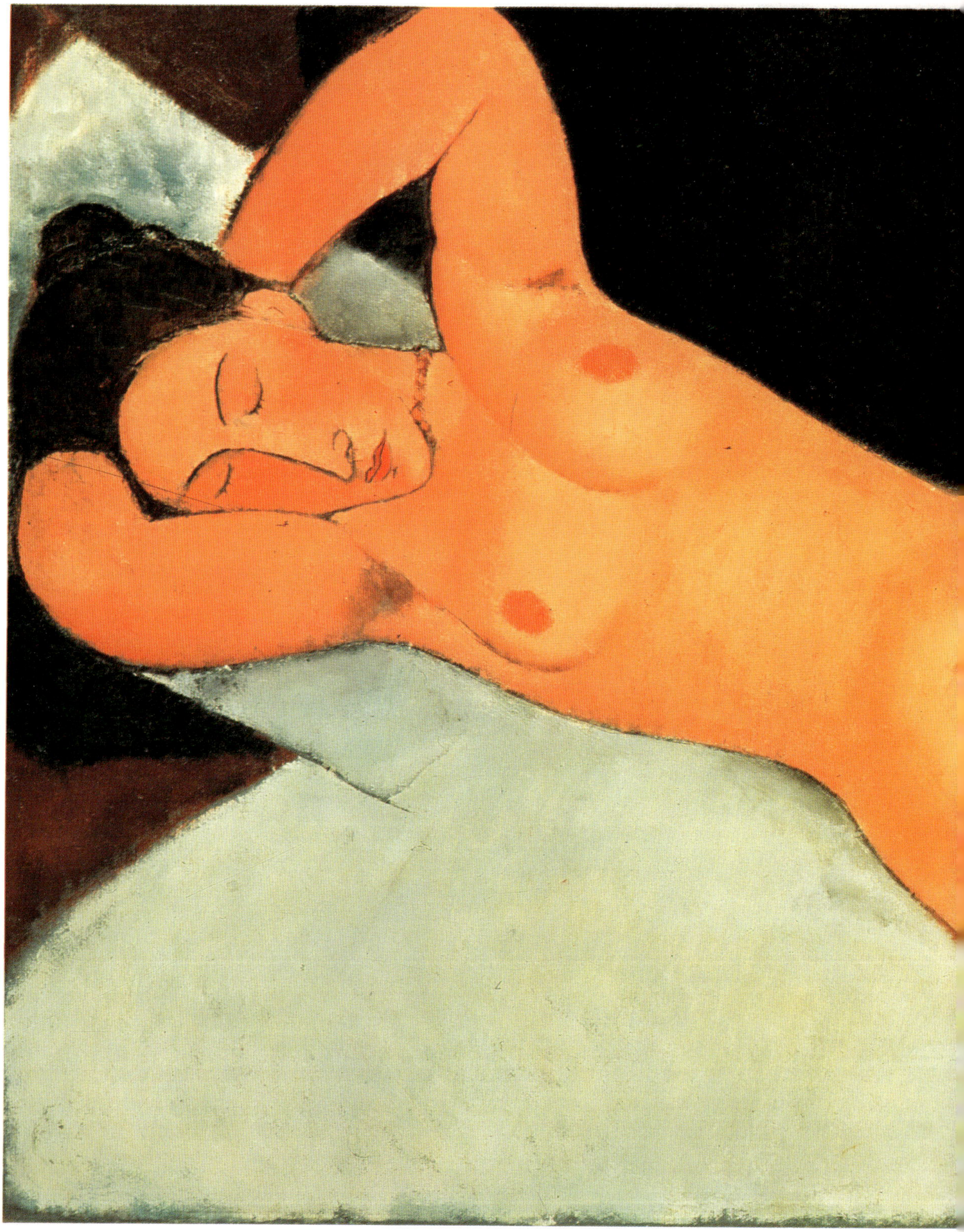

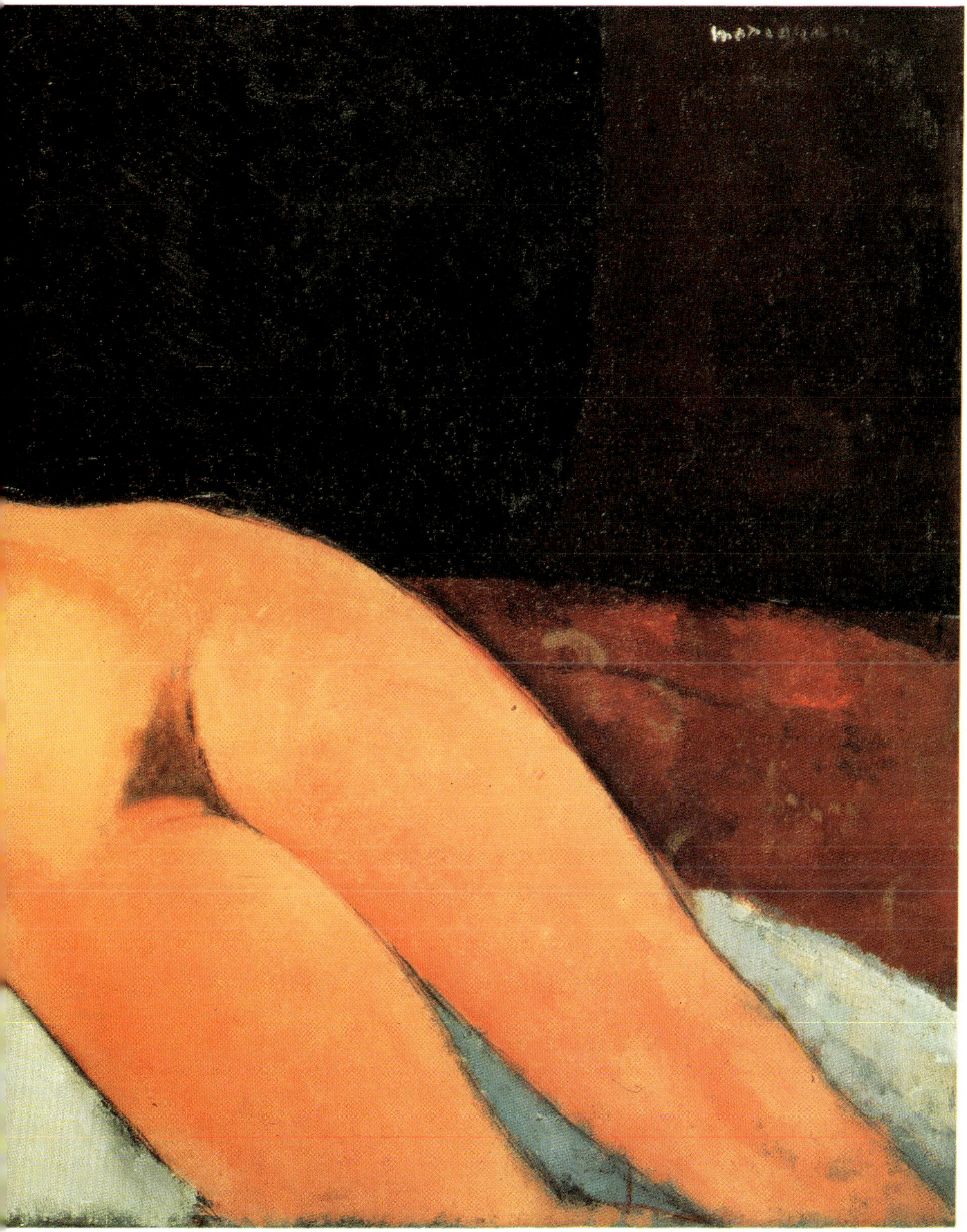

Nude with Necklace, her Eyes Closed

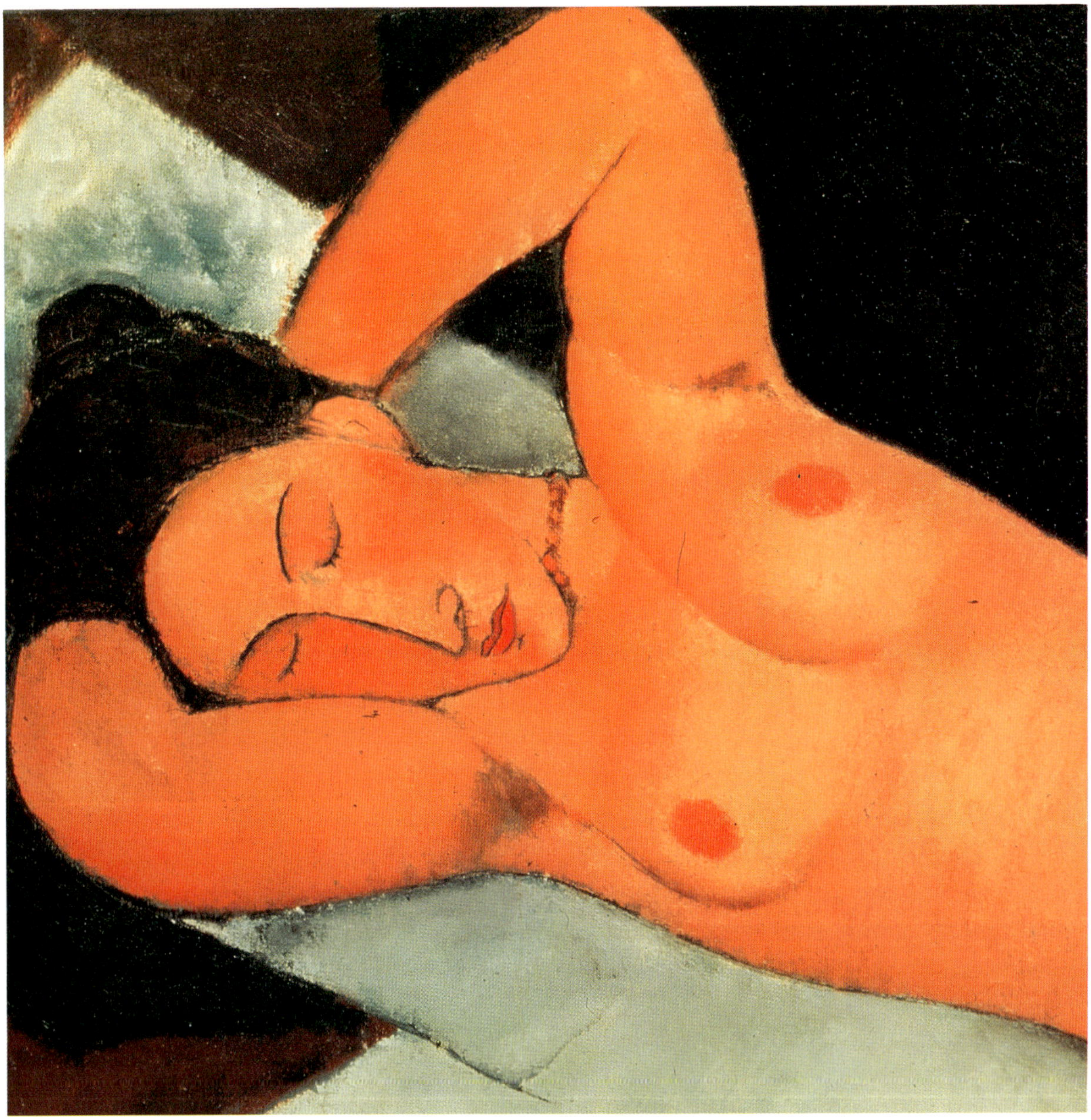

Nude with Necklace, her Eyes Closed (Detail)

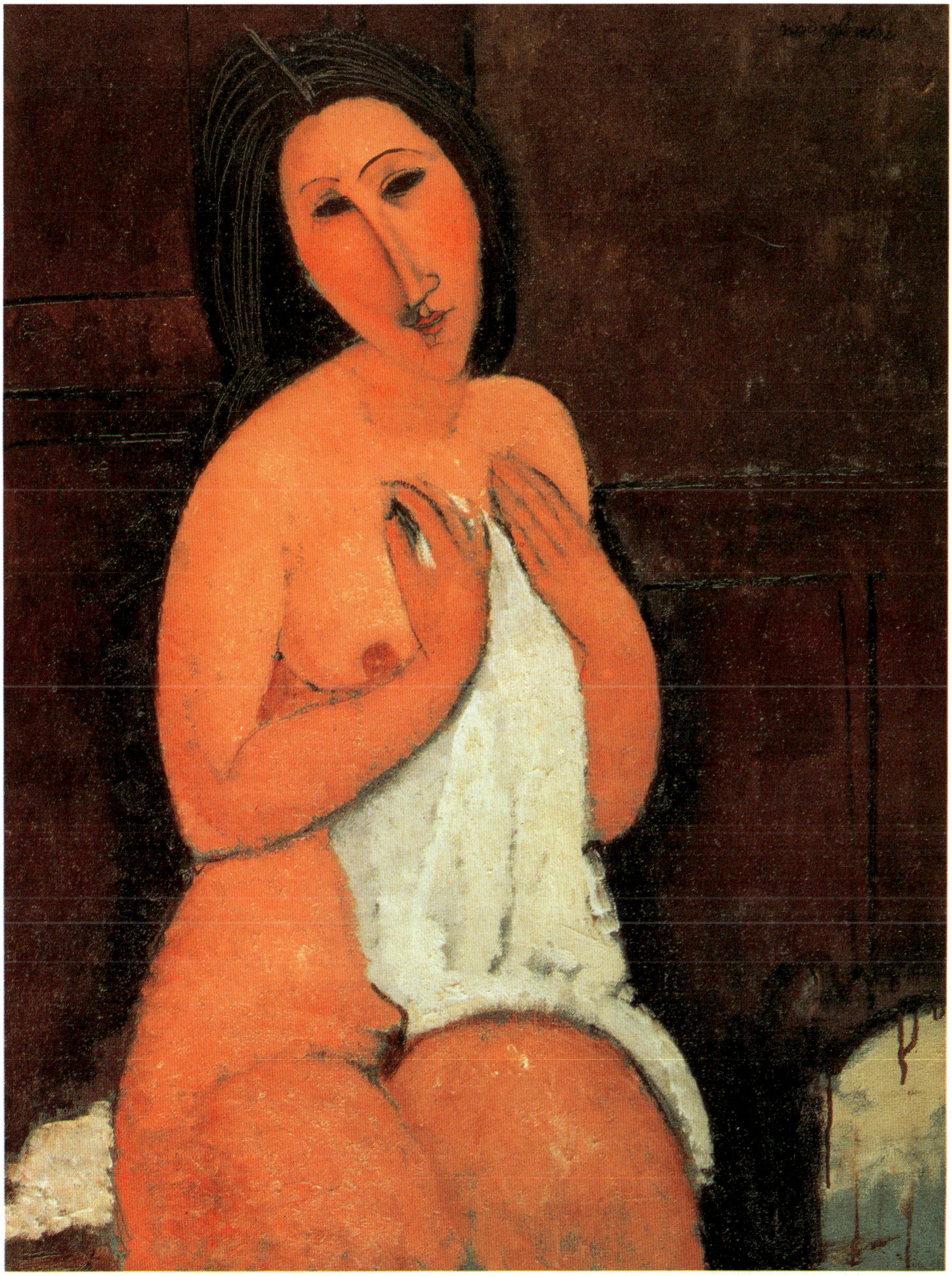

Seated Nude with a Shirt

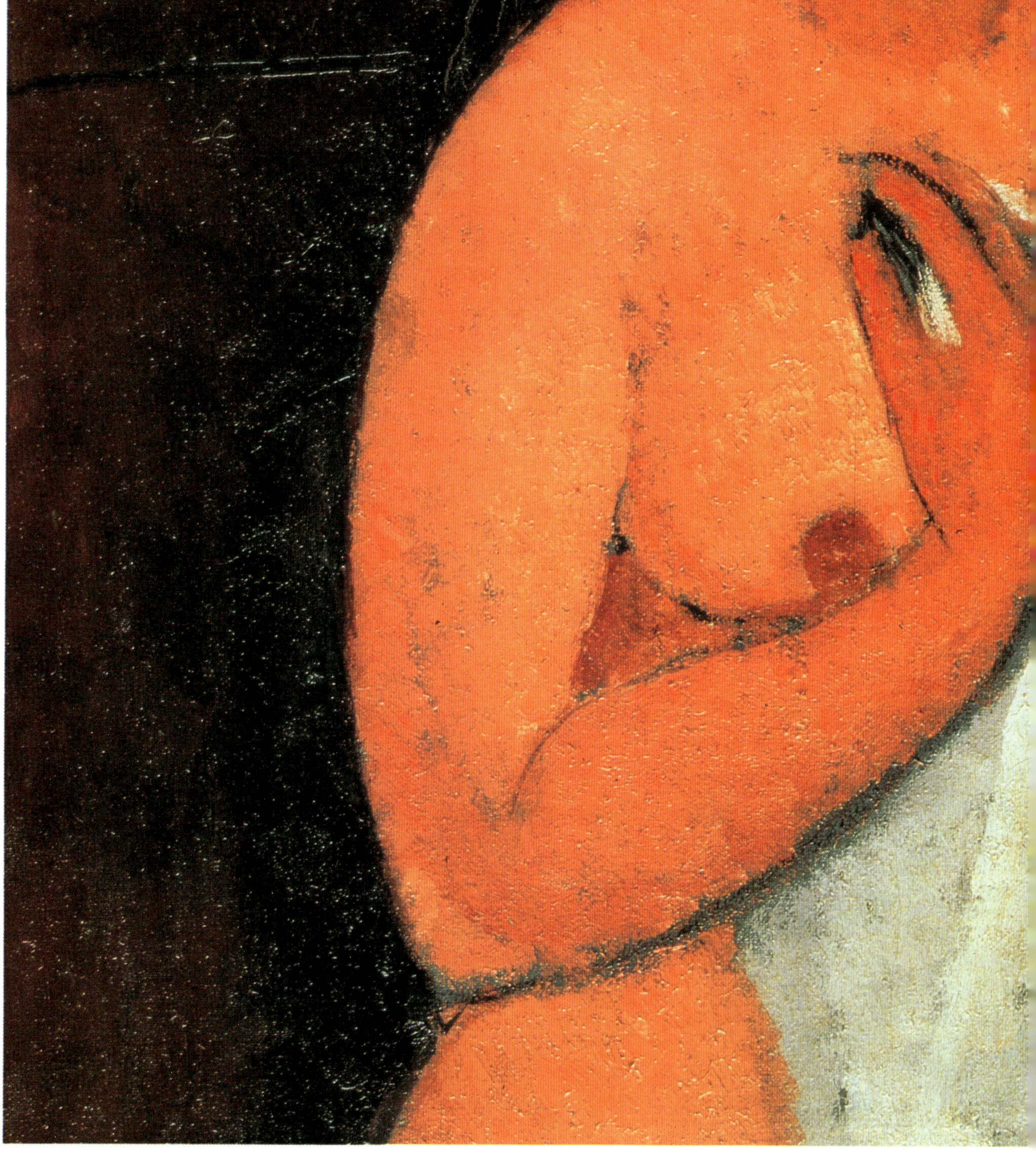

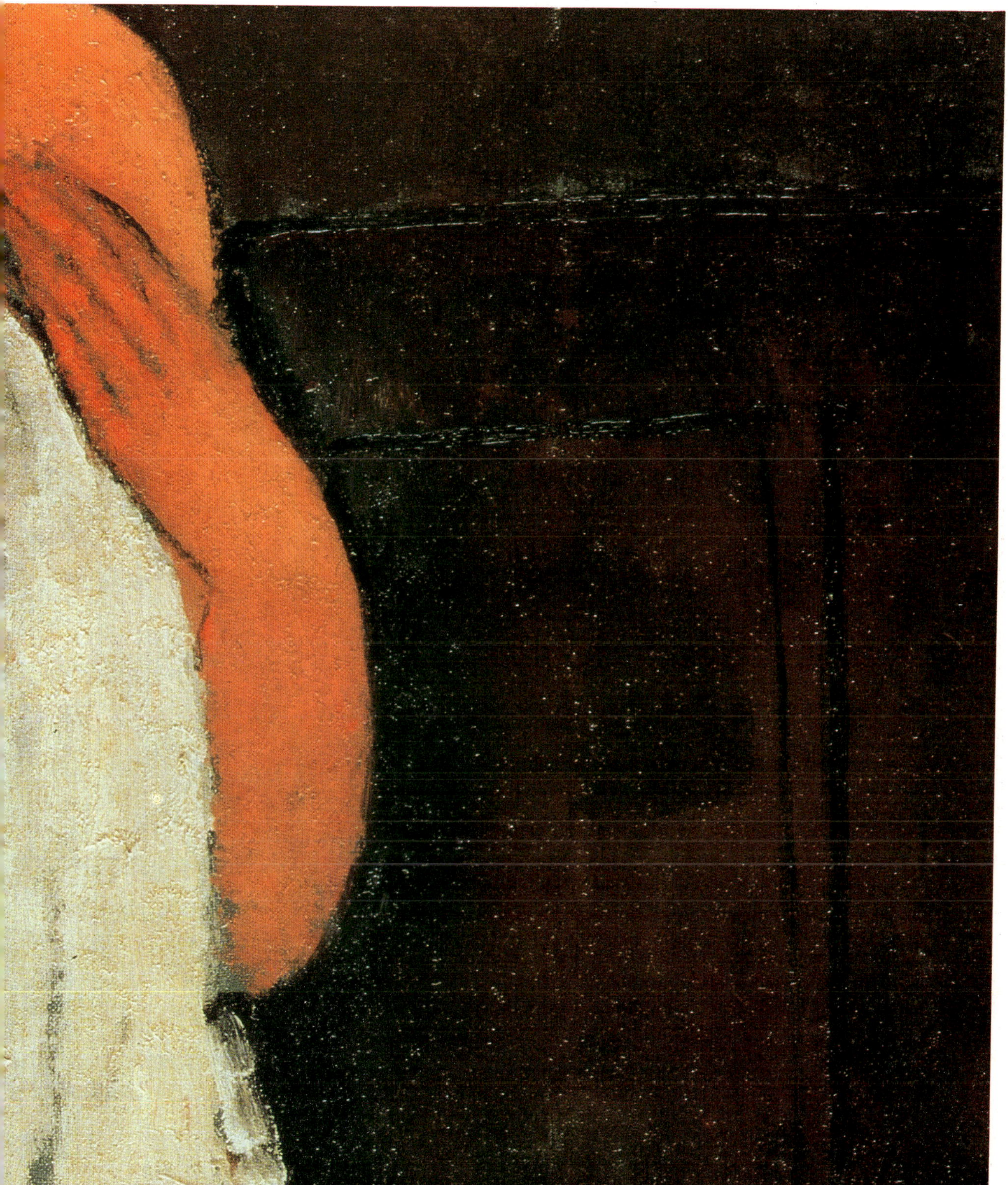

Seated Nude with a Shirt (Detail)

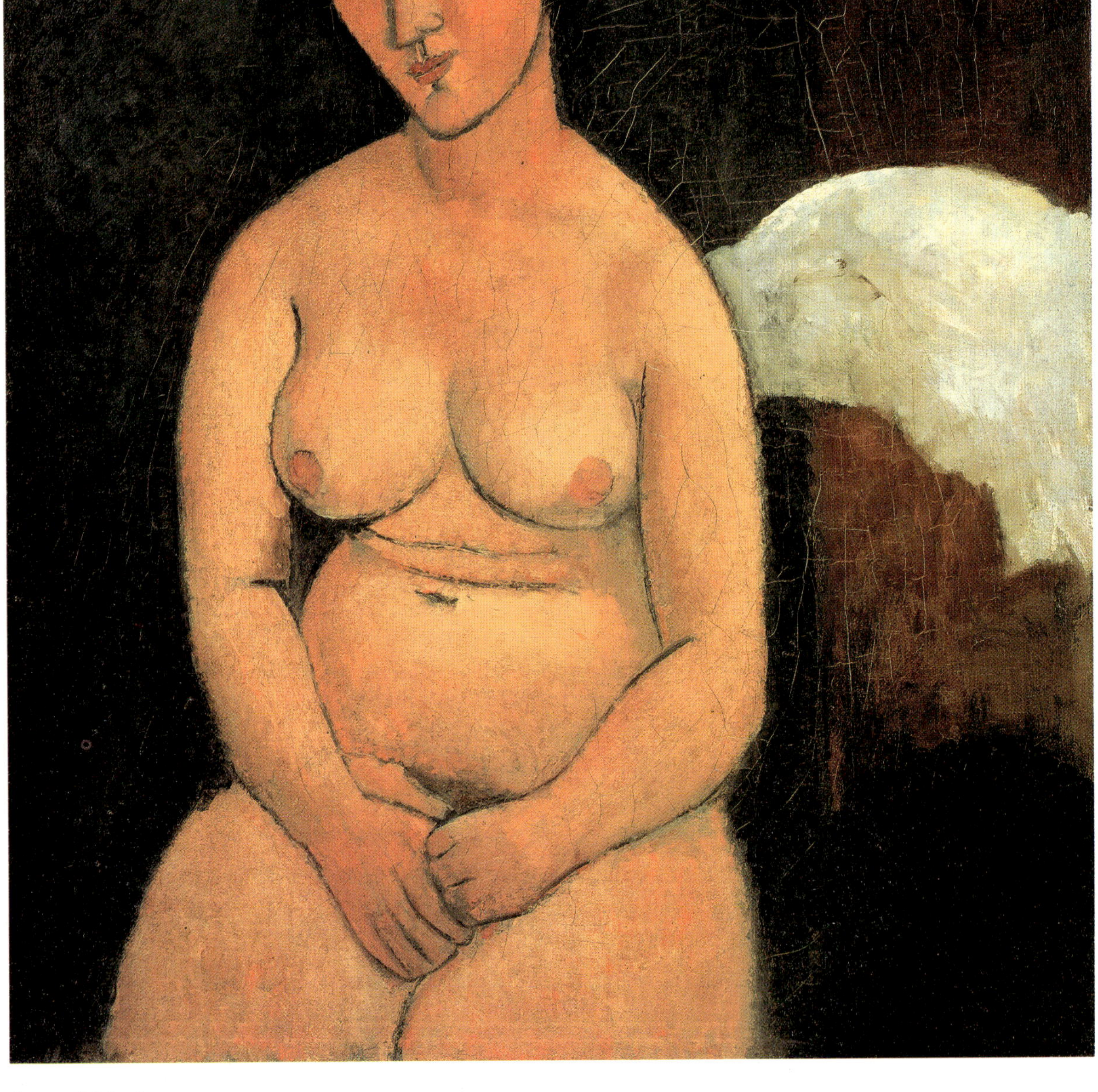

Seated Nude

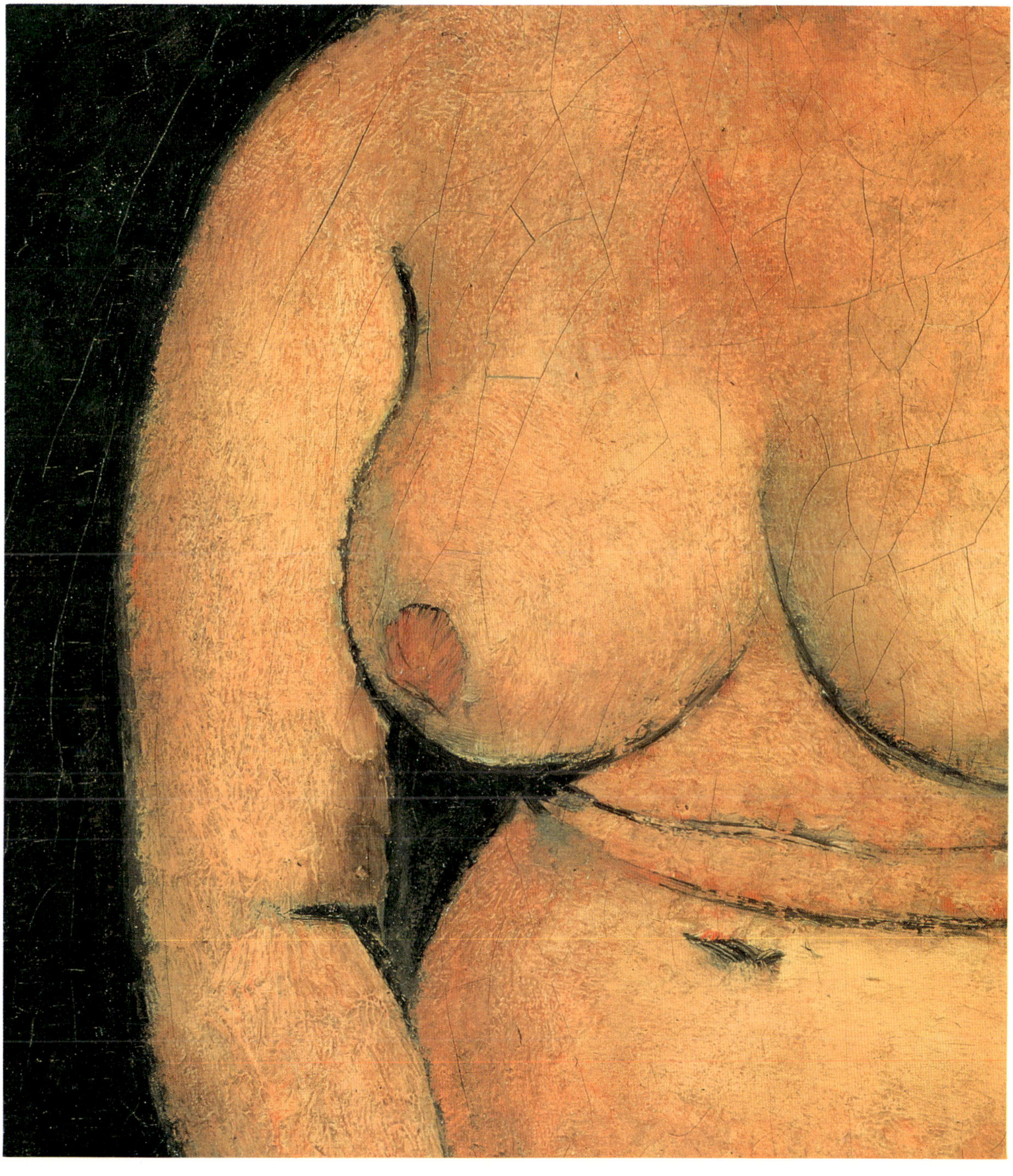

Seated Nude (Detail)

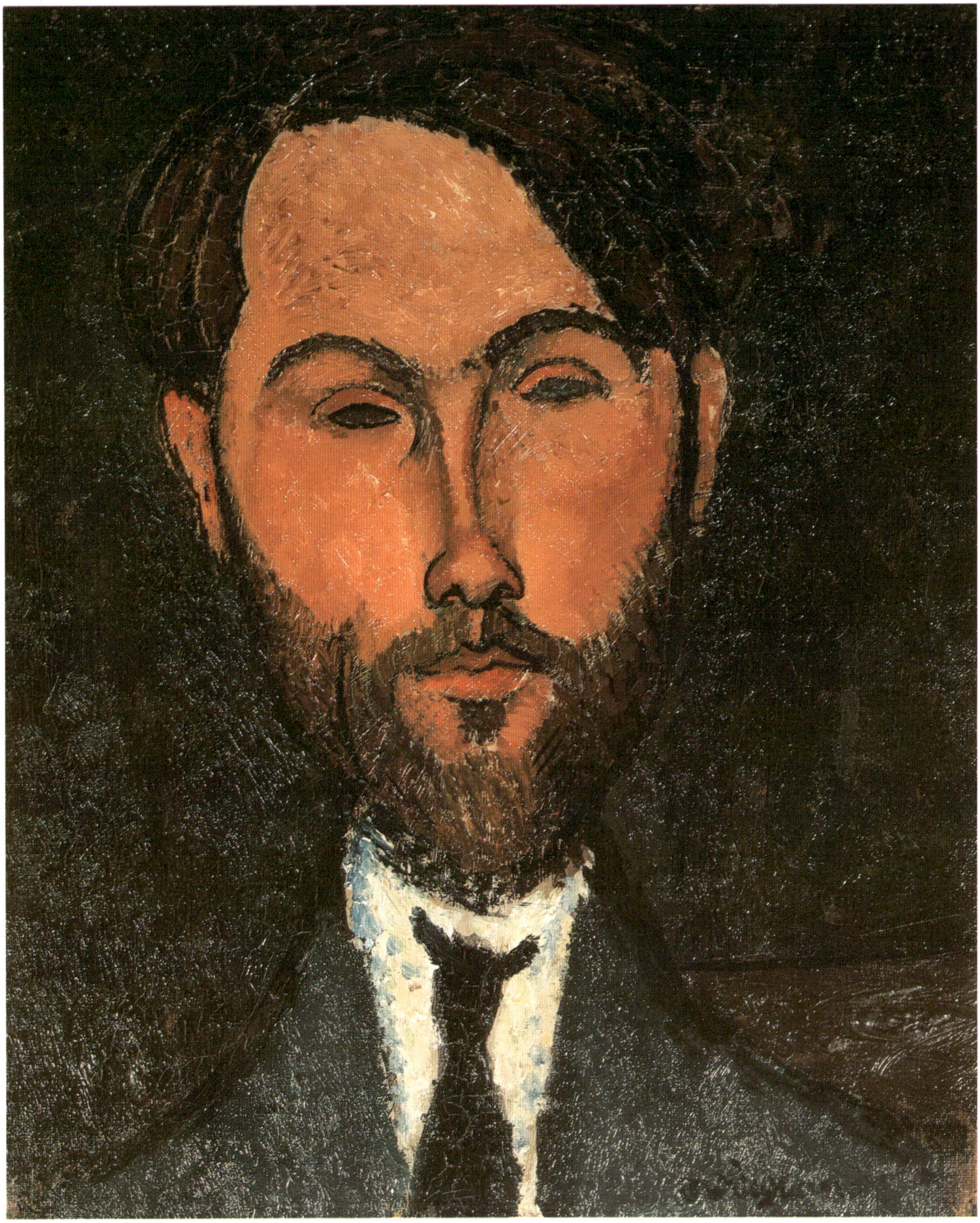

Léopold Zborowski

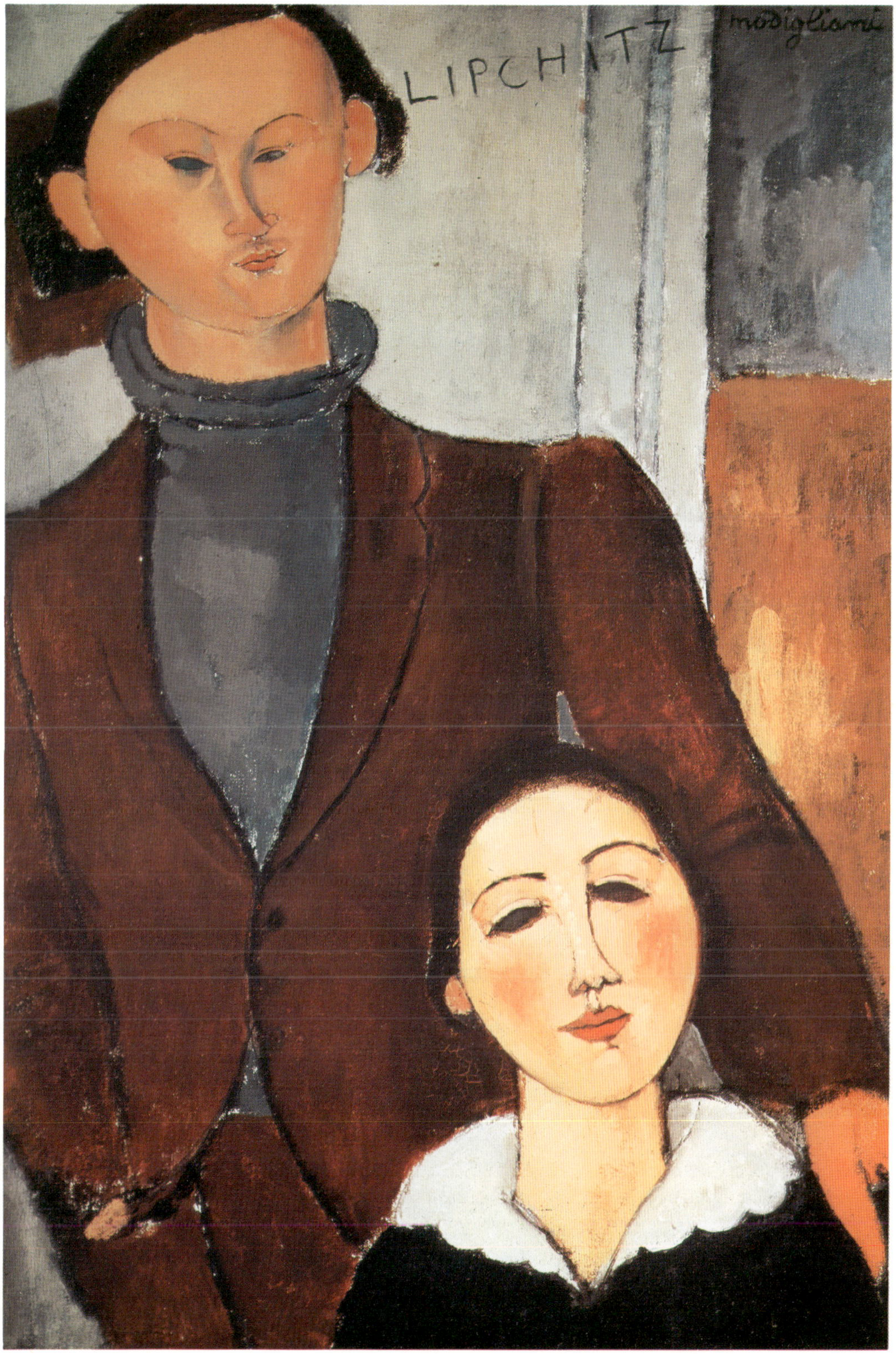

Jacques Lipchitz and His Wife

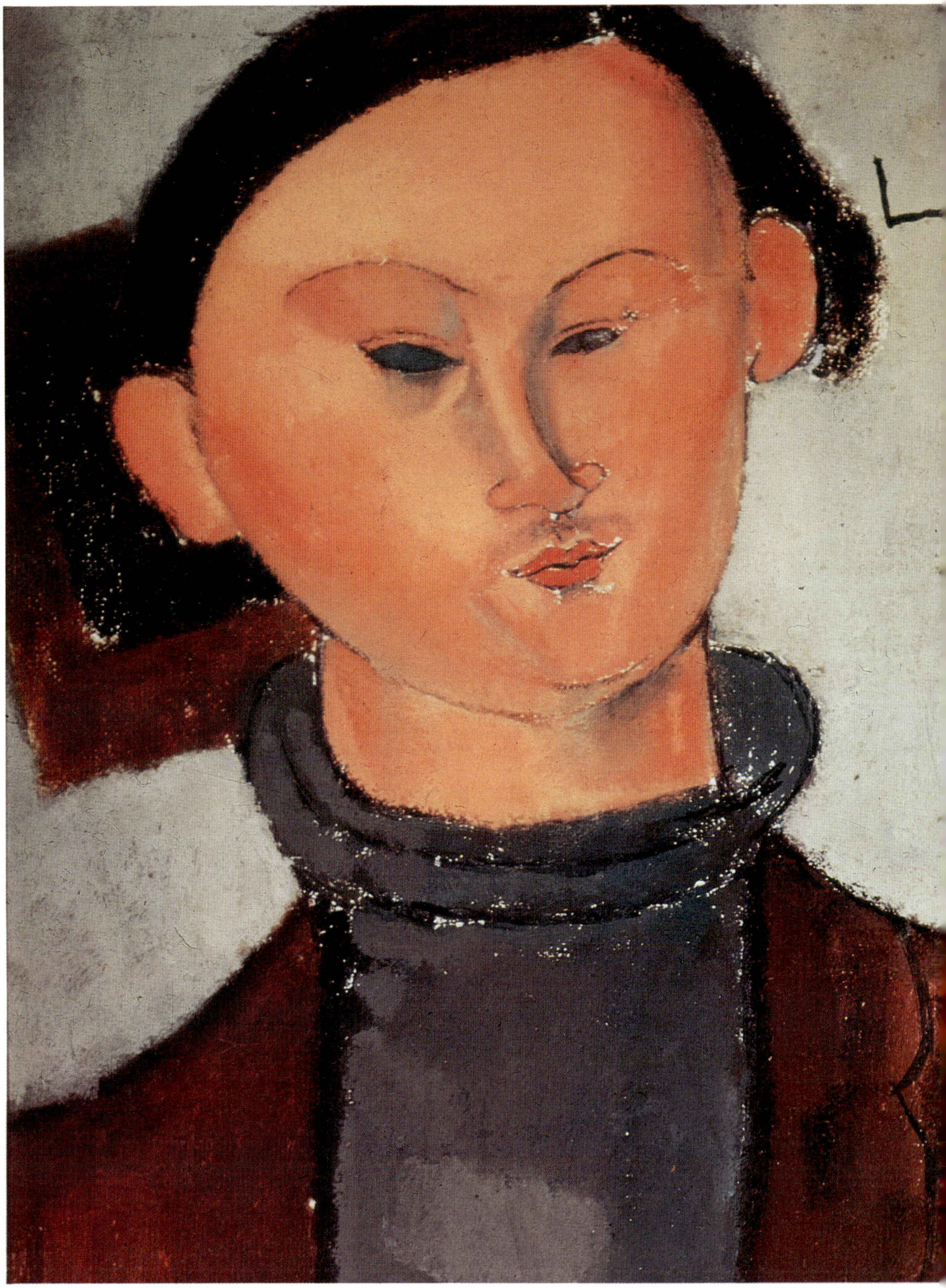

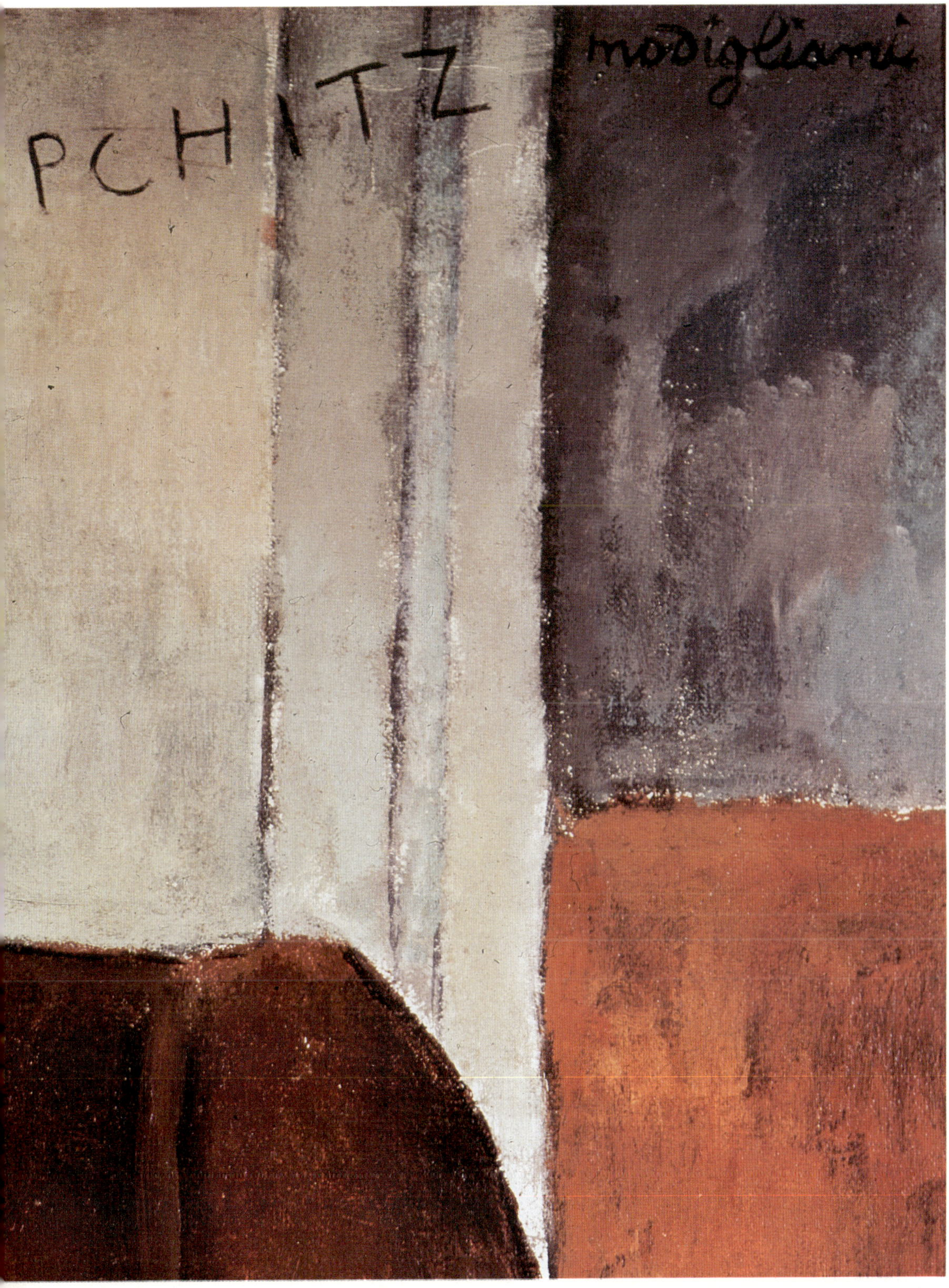

Jacques Lipchitz and His Wife (Detail)

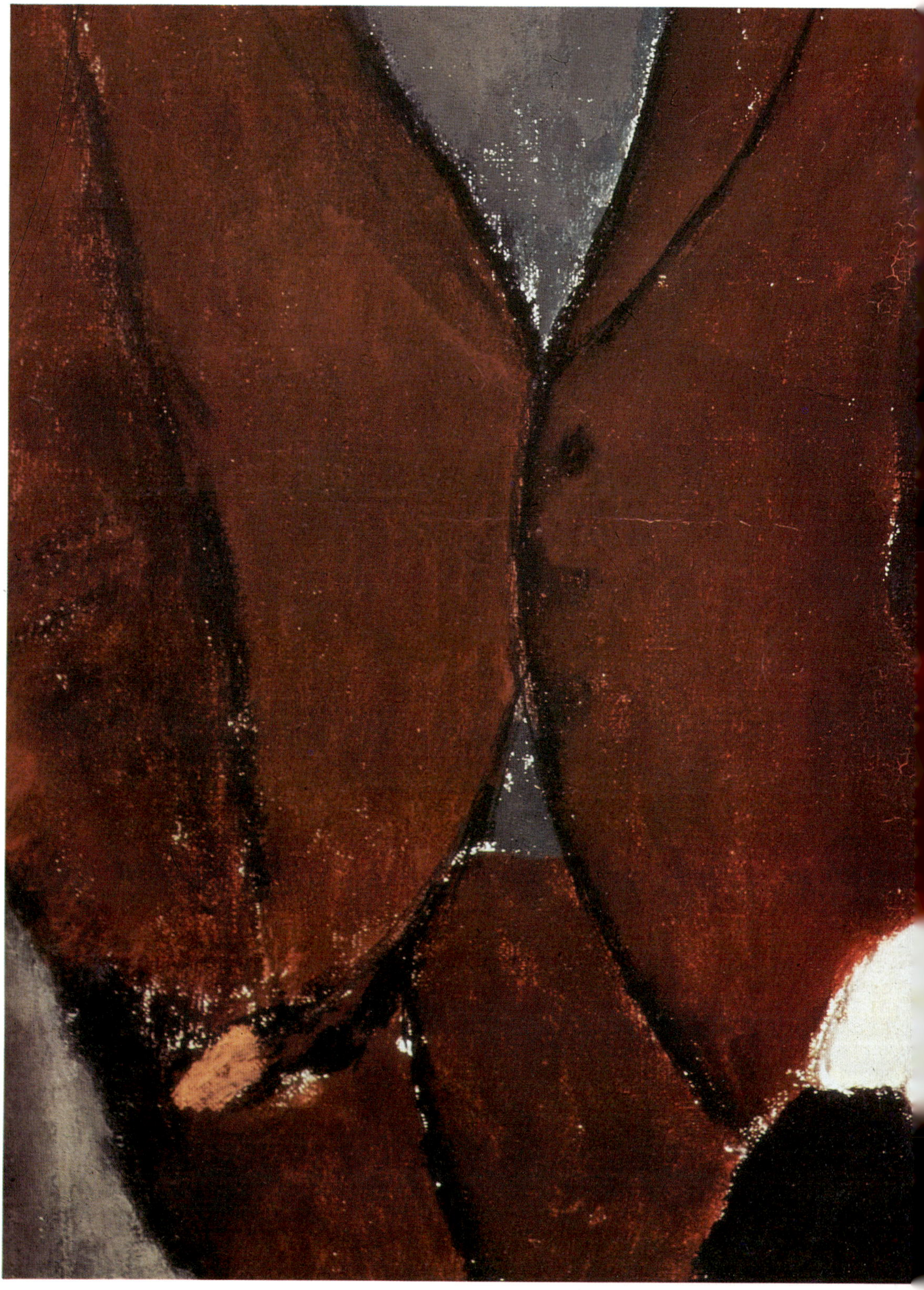

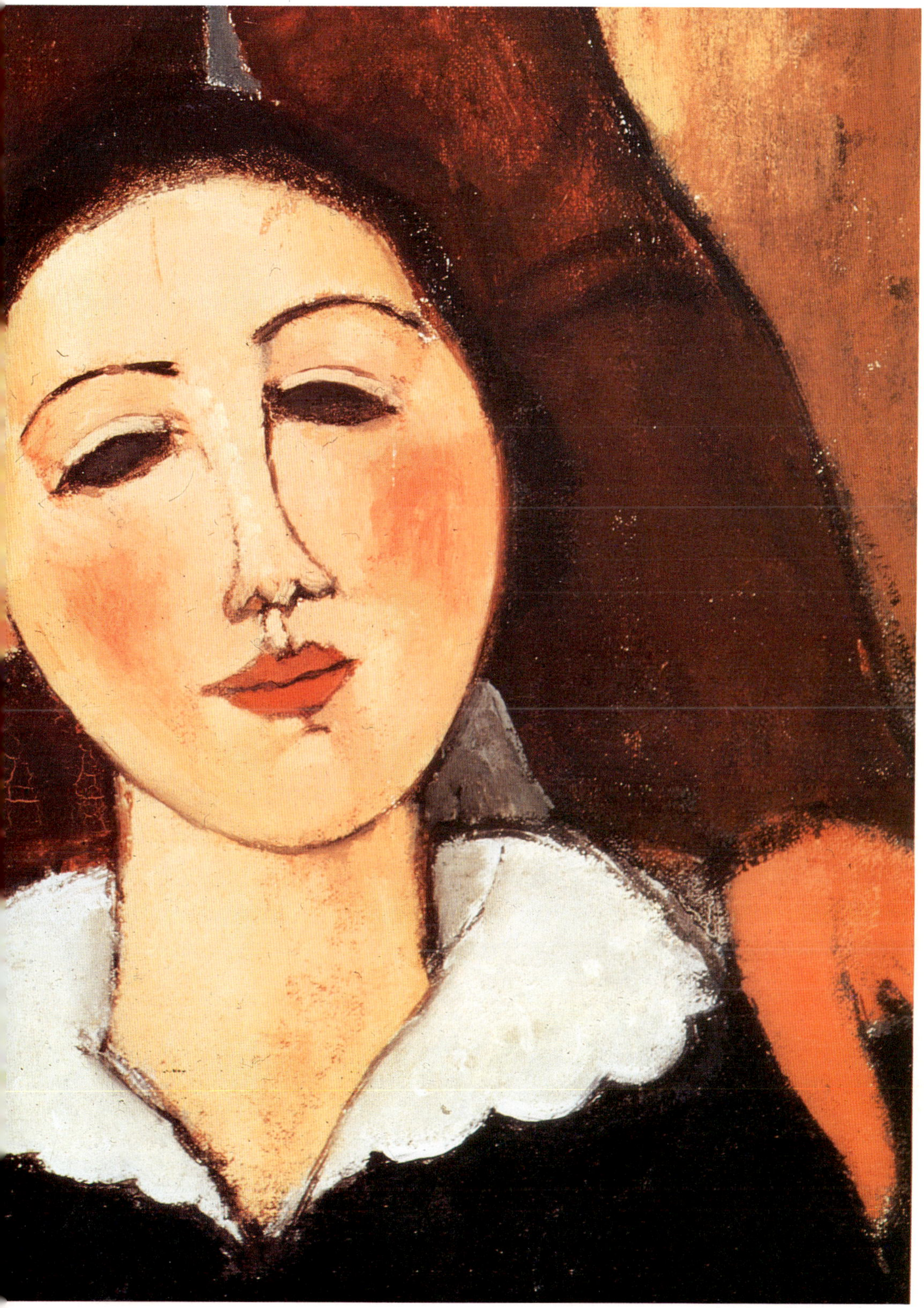

Jacques Lipchitz and His Wife (Detail)

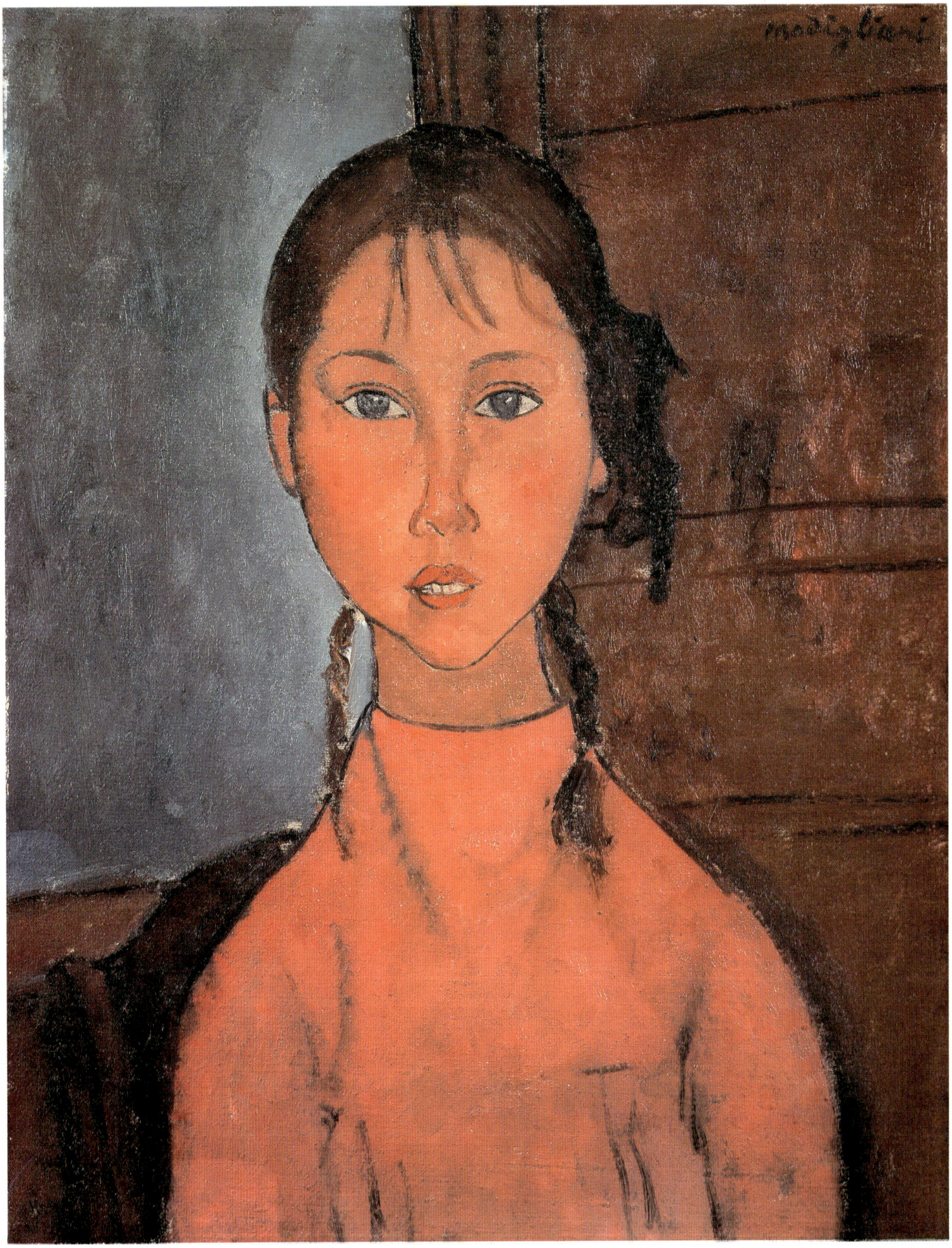

Girl with Braids

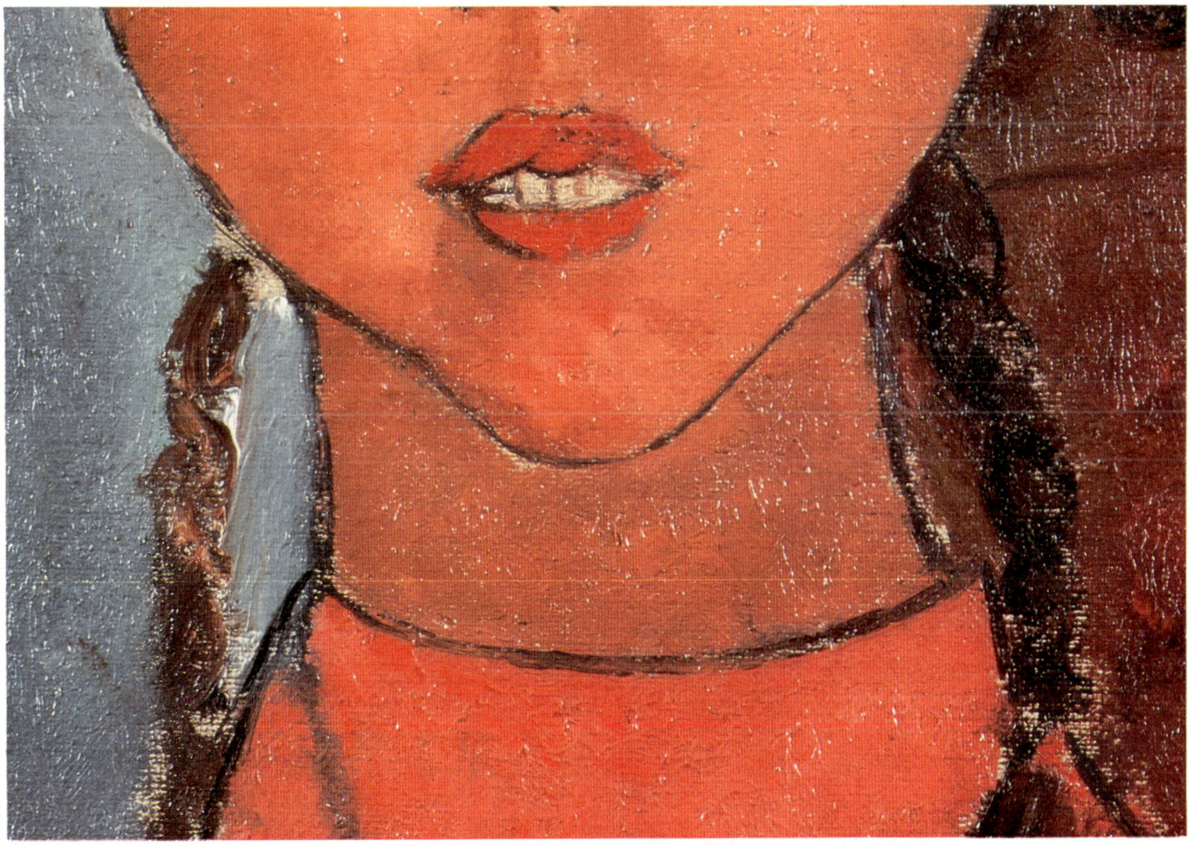

Girl with Braids (Detail)

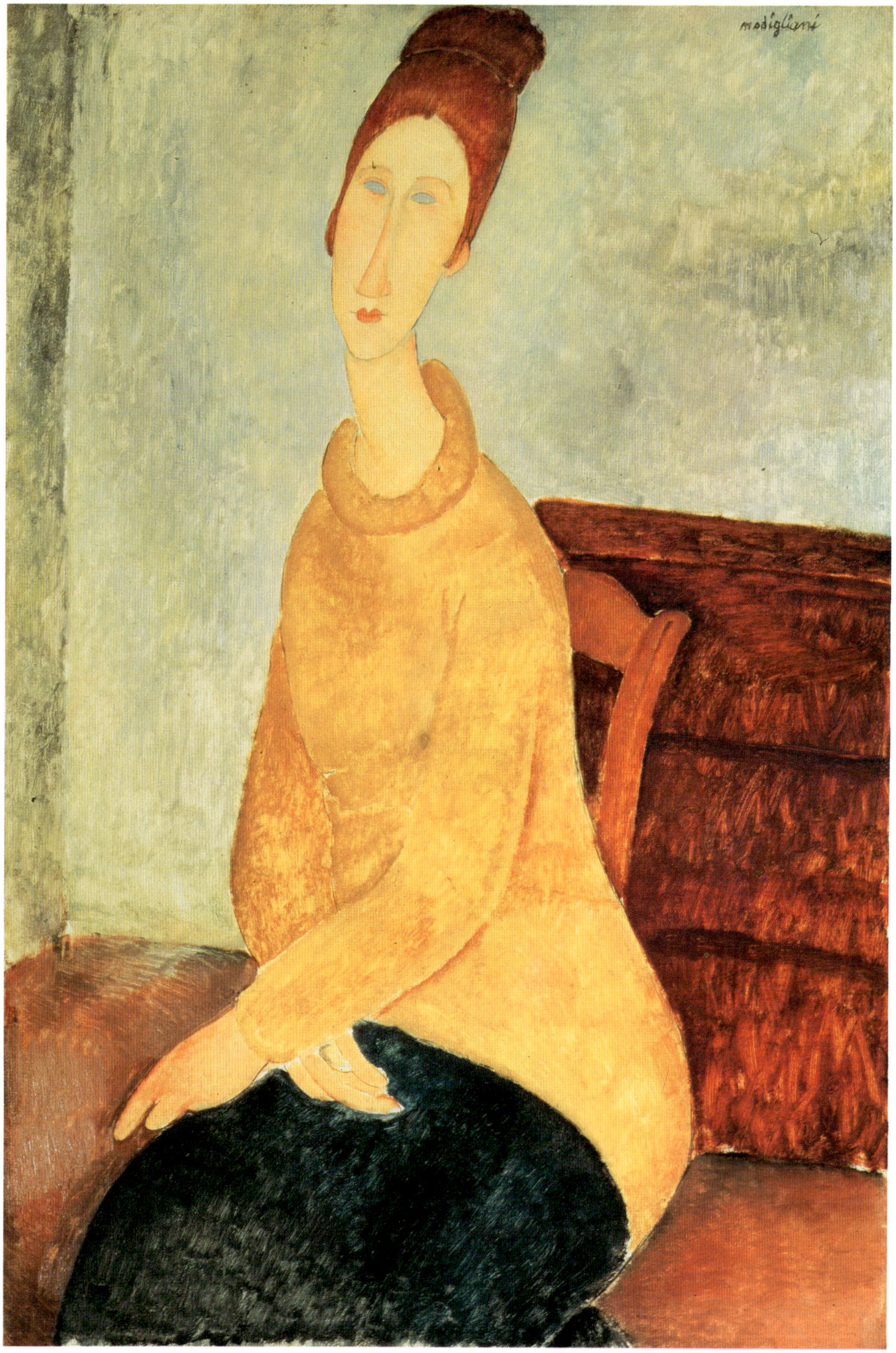

Yellow Sweater (Portrait of Mademoiselle Hébuterne)

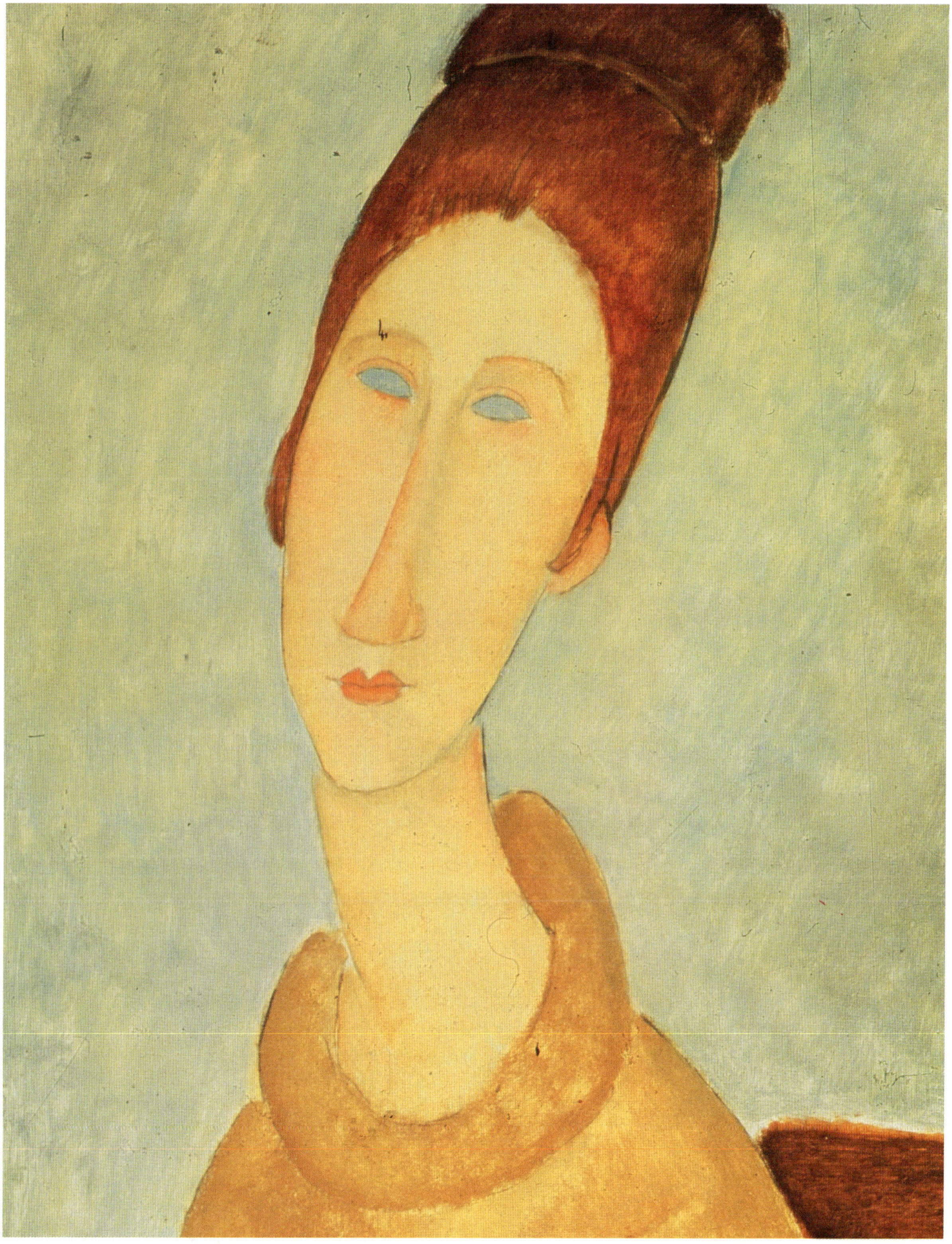

Yellow Sweater (Detail)

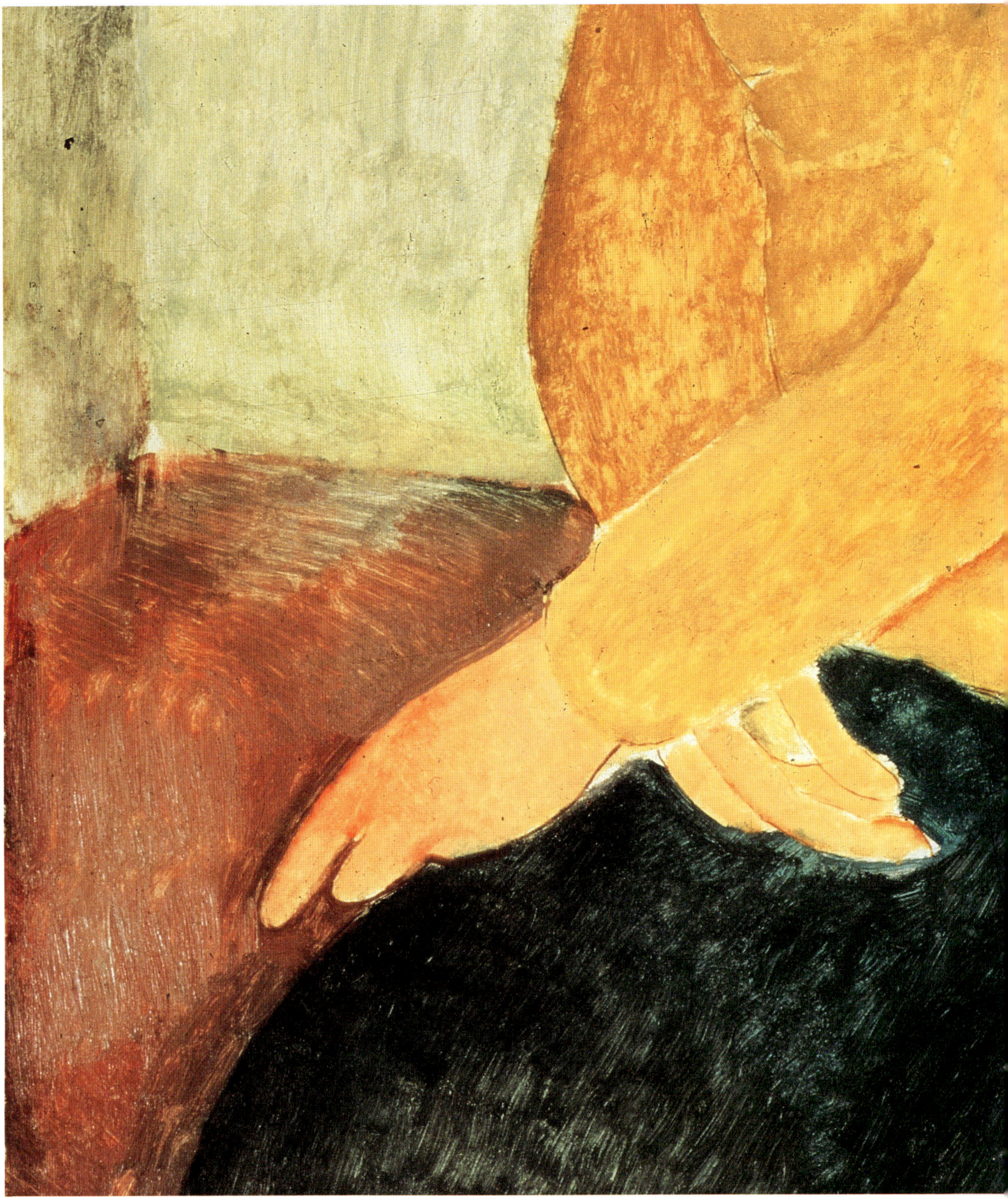

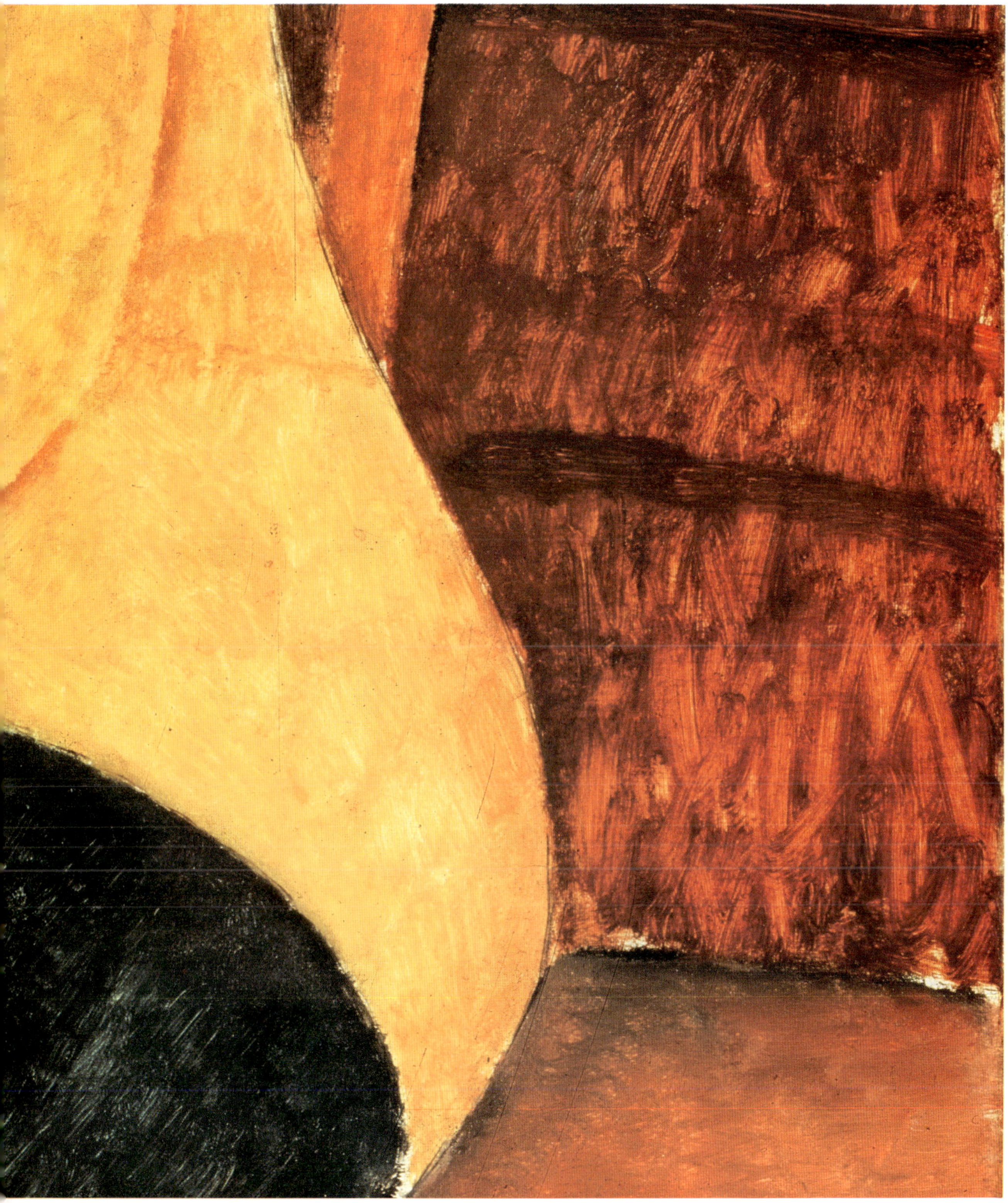

Yellow Sweater (Detail)

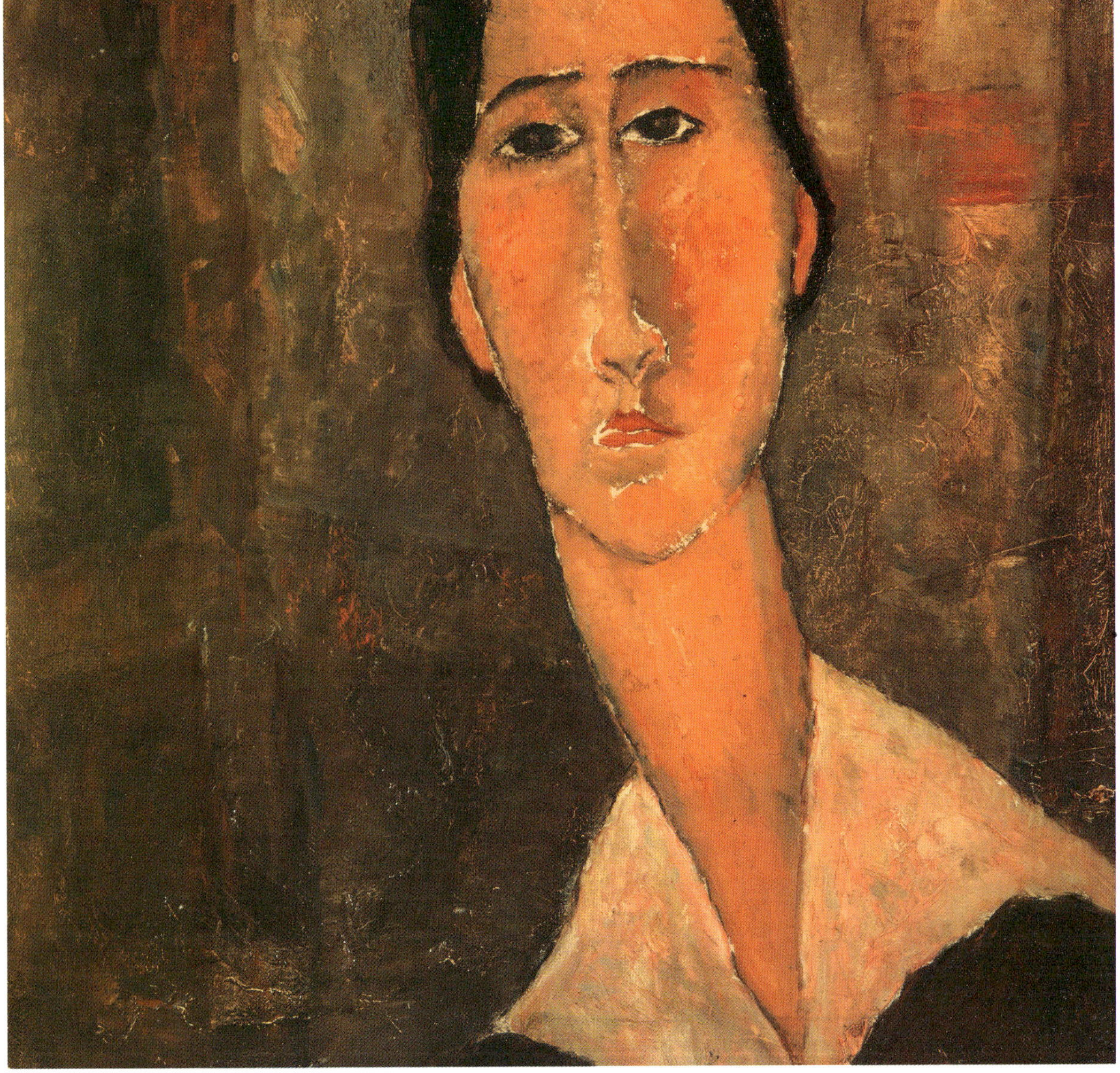

Jeanne Hébuterne with White Collar

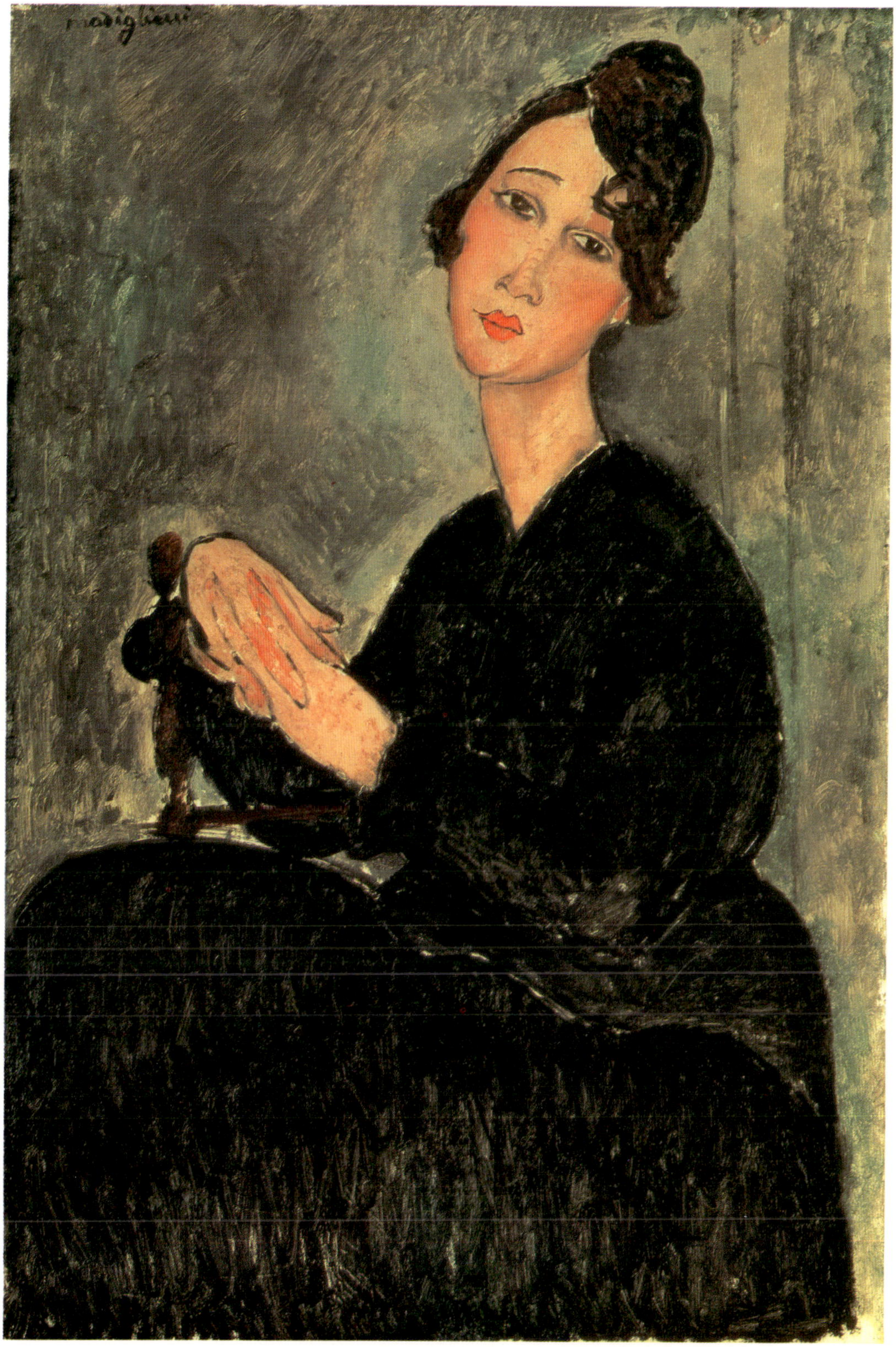

Portrait of Dédie (dedicated to Odette Hayden)

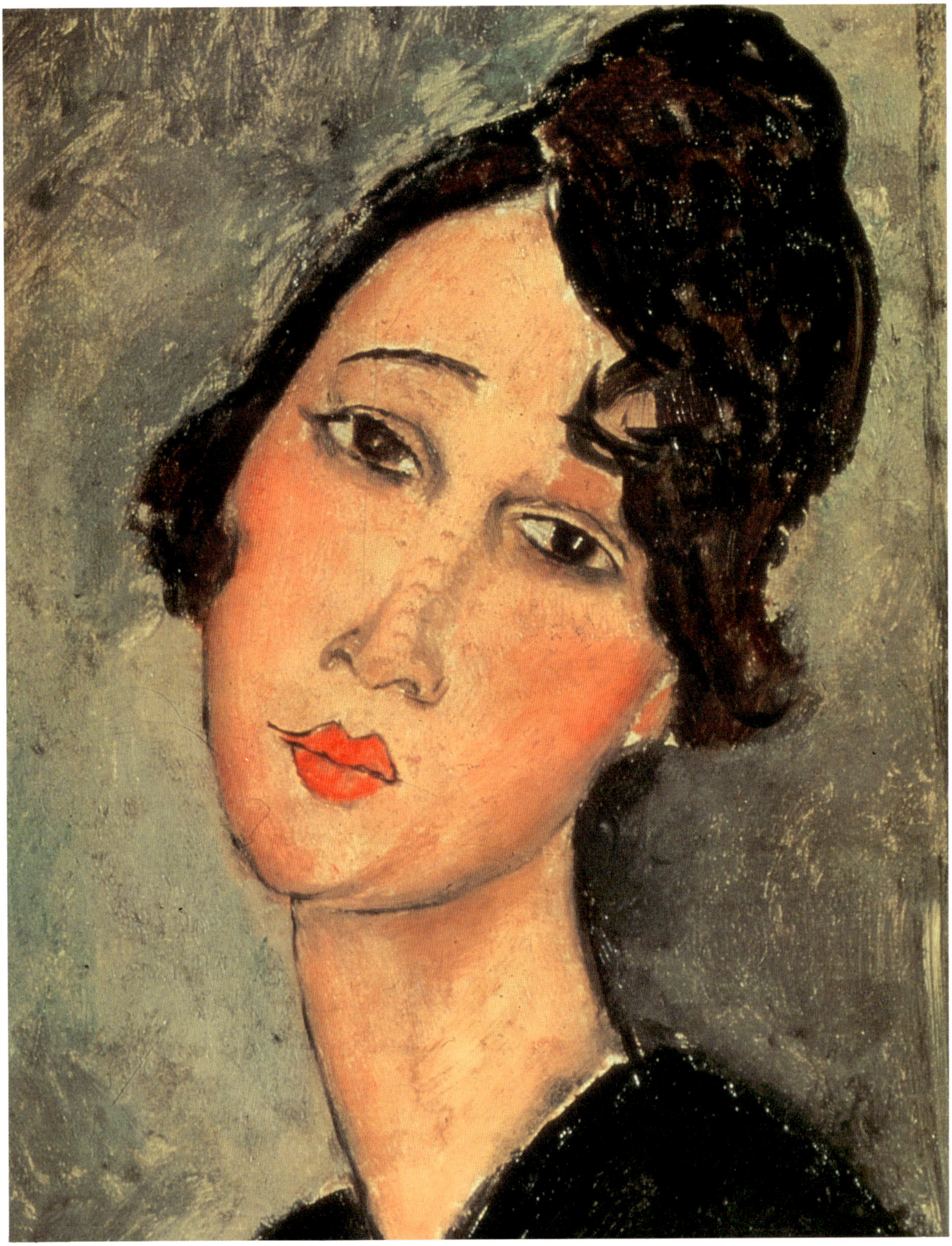

Portrait of Dédie (dedicated to Odette Hayden) (Detail)

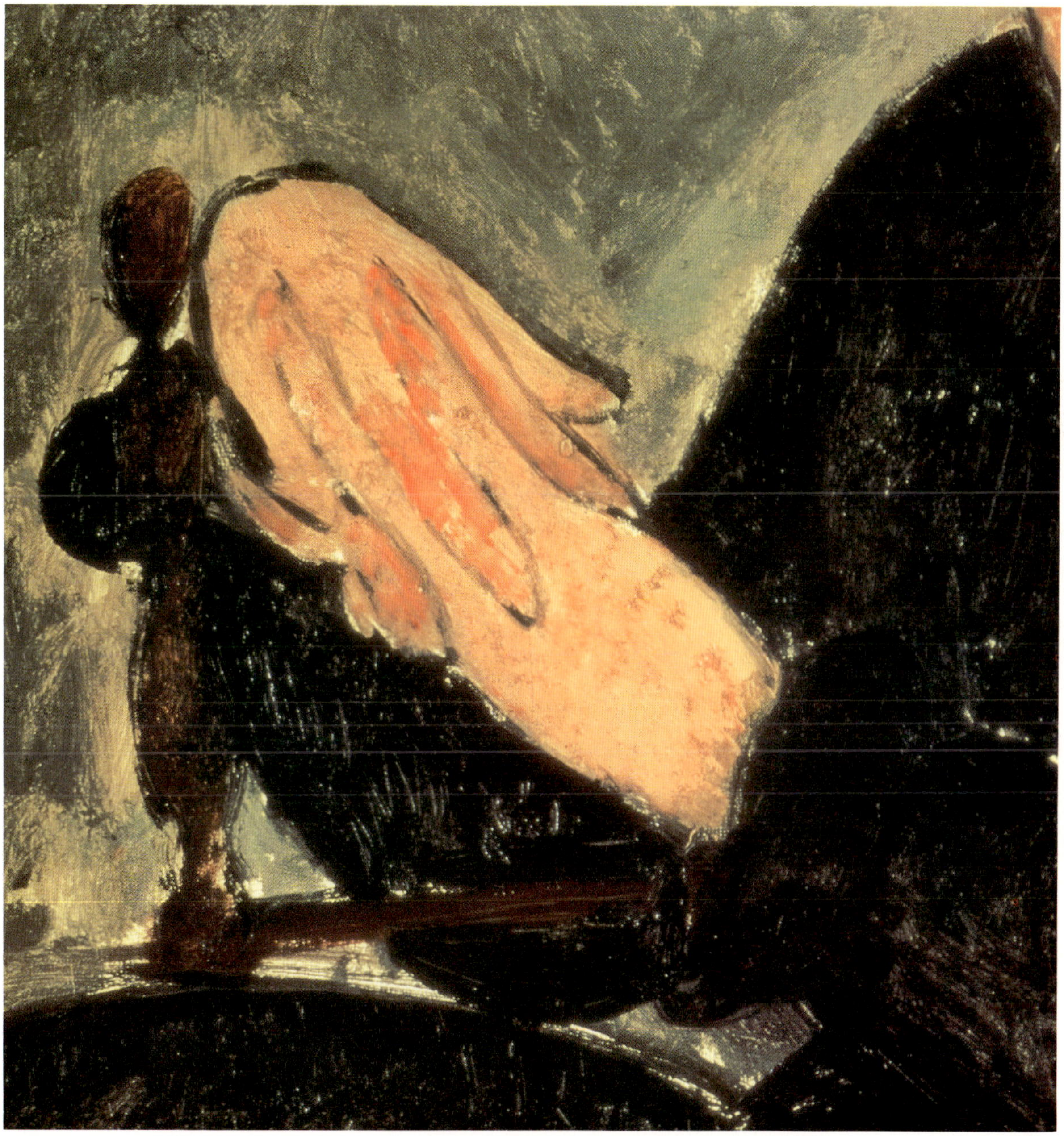

Portrait of Dédie (dedicated to Odette Hayden) (Detail)

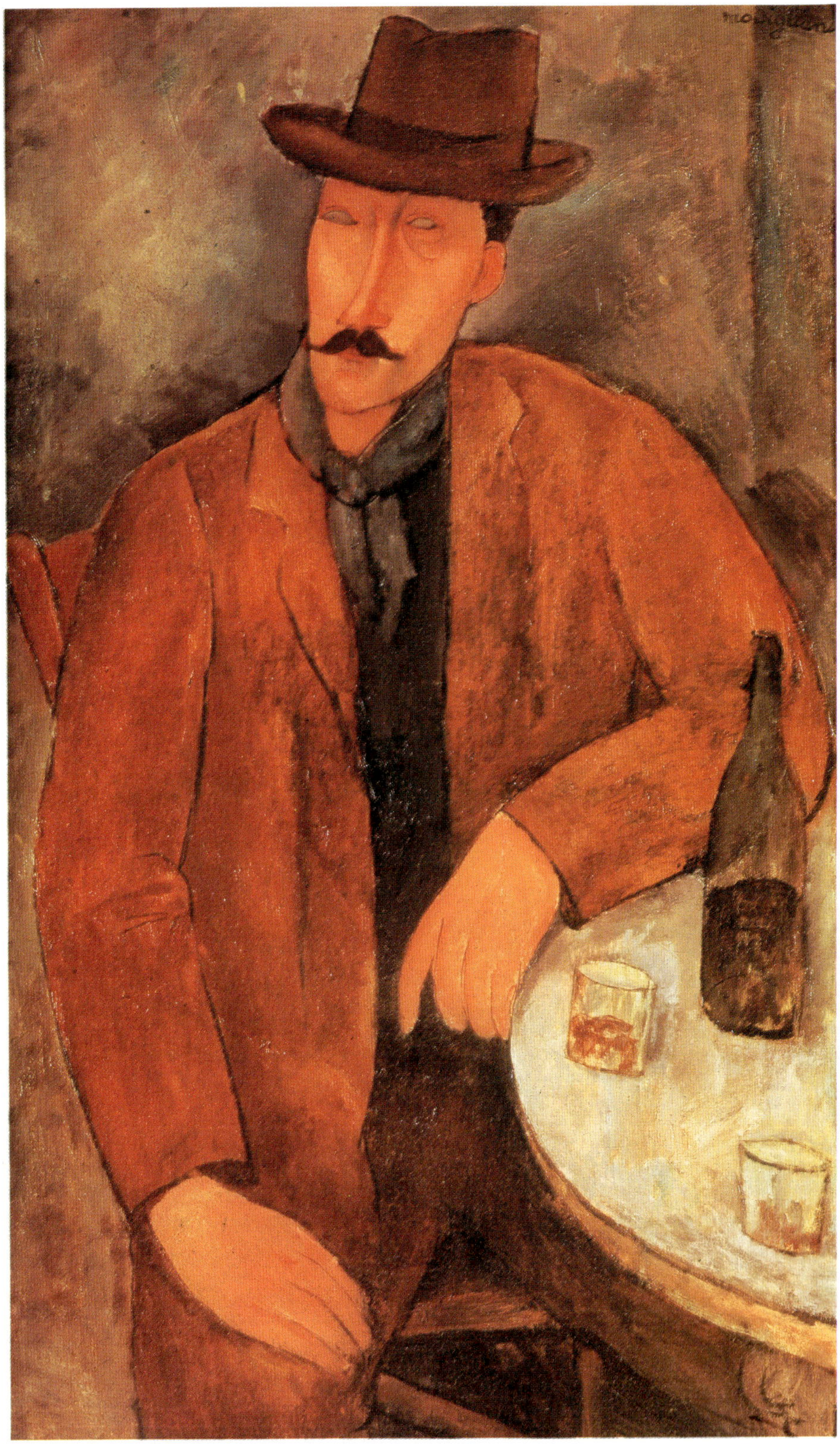

Man Leaning on a Table

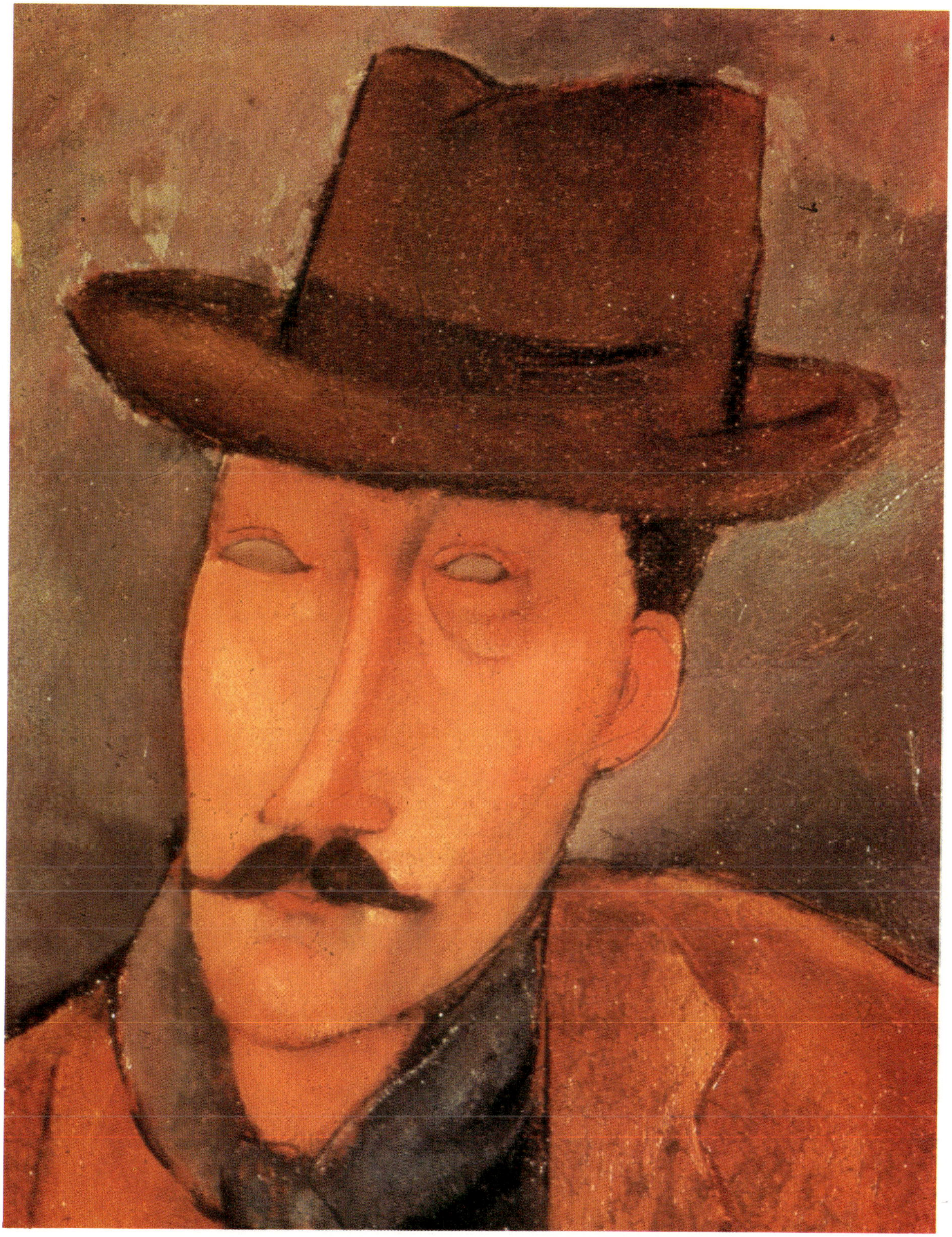

Man Leaning on a Table (Detail)

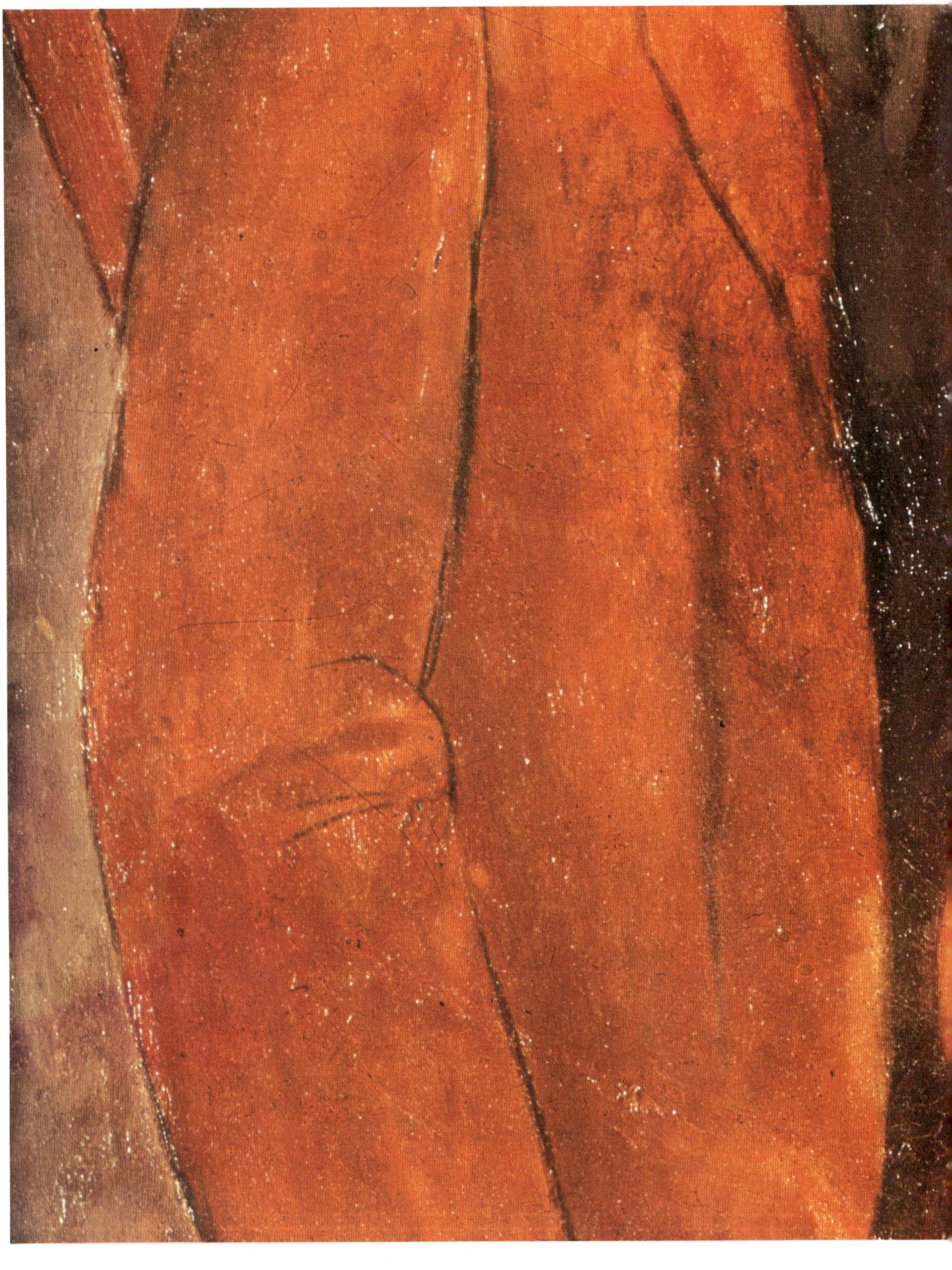

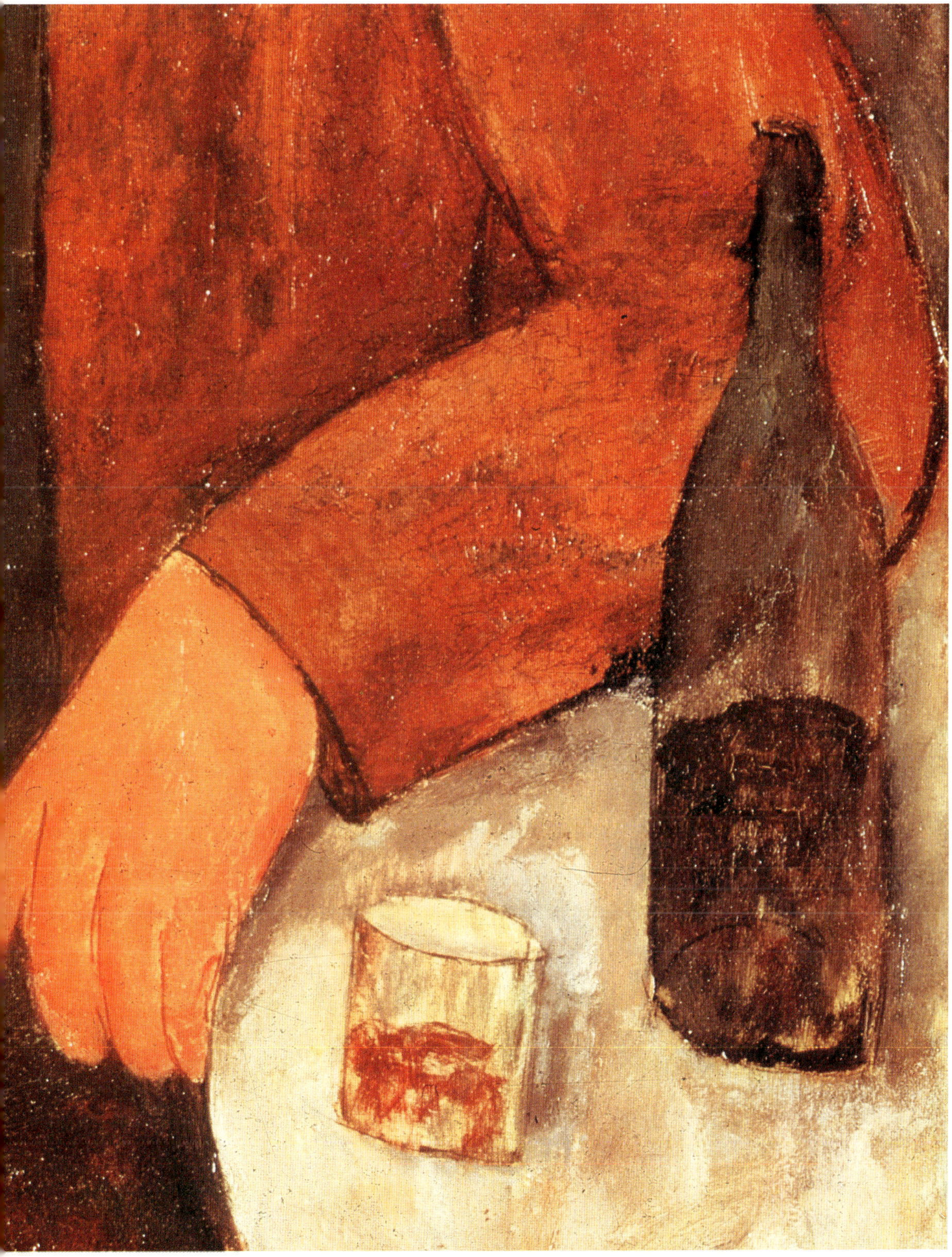

Man Leaning on a Table (Detail)

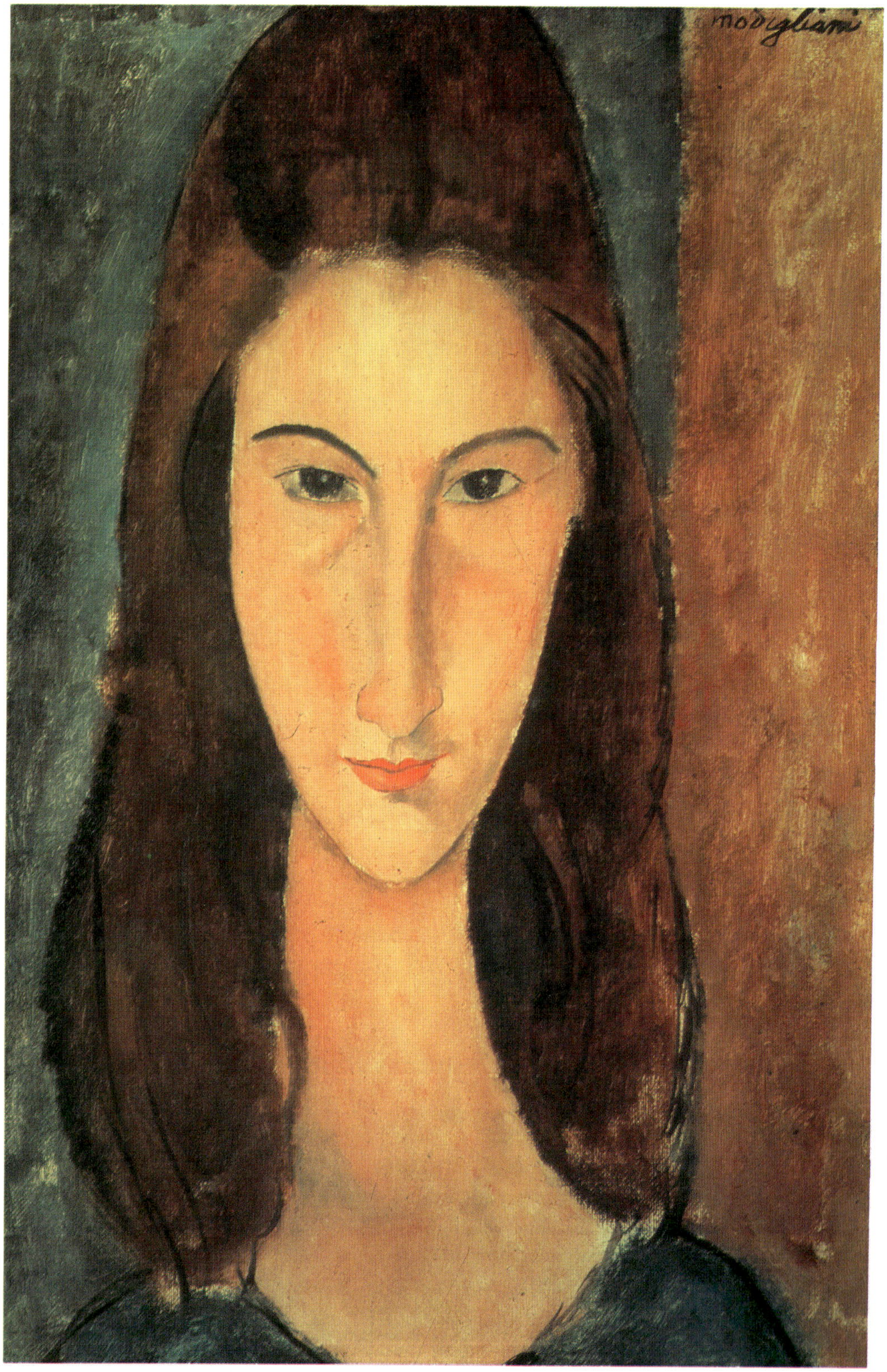

Jeanne Hébuterne

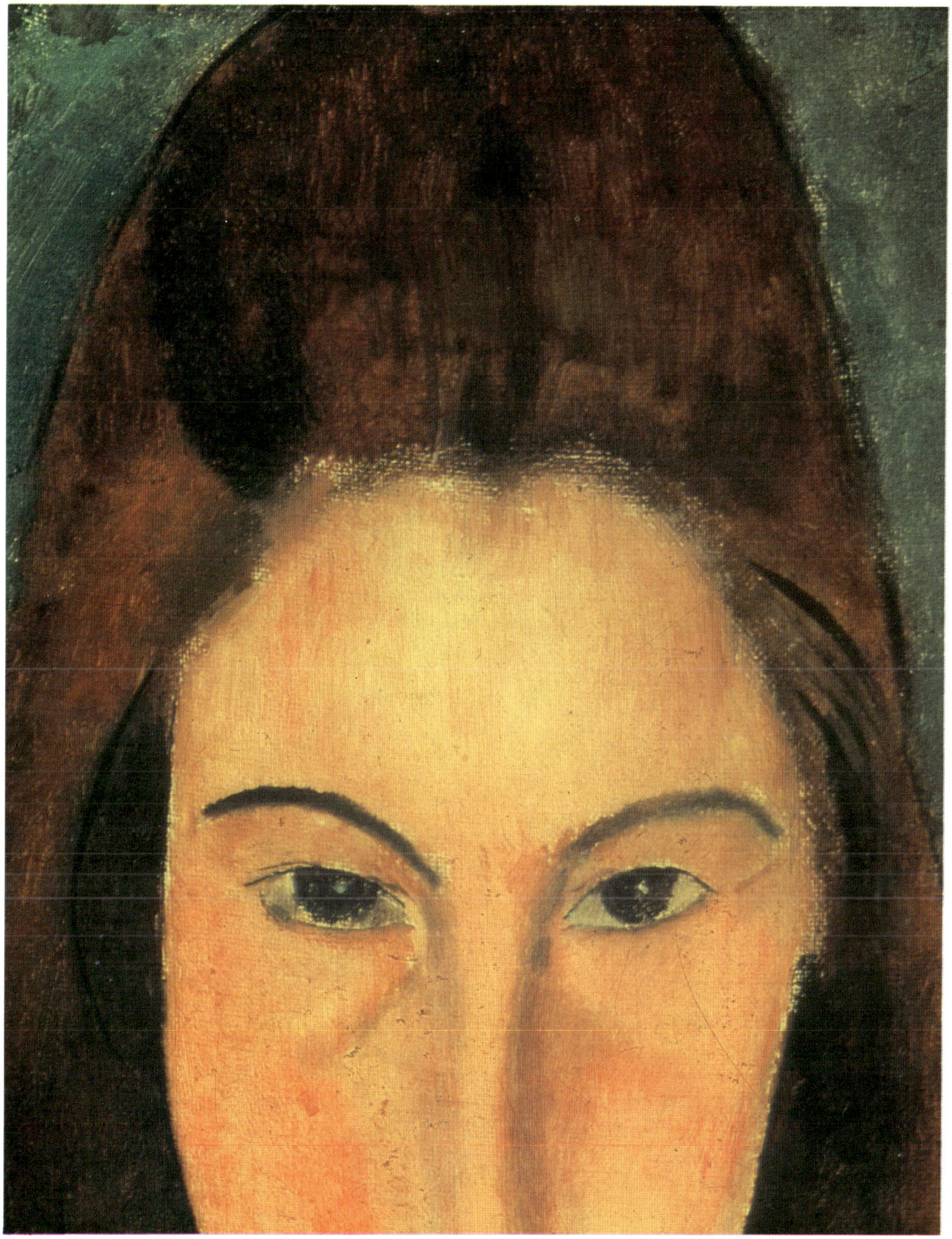

Jeanne Hébuterne (Detail)

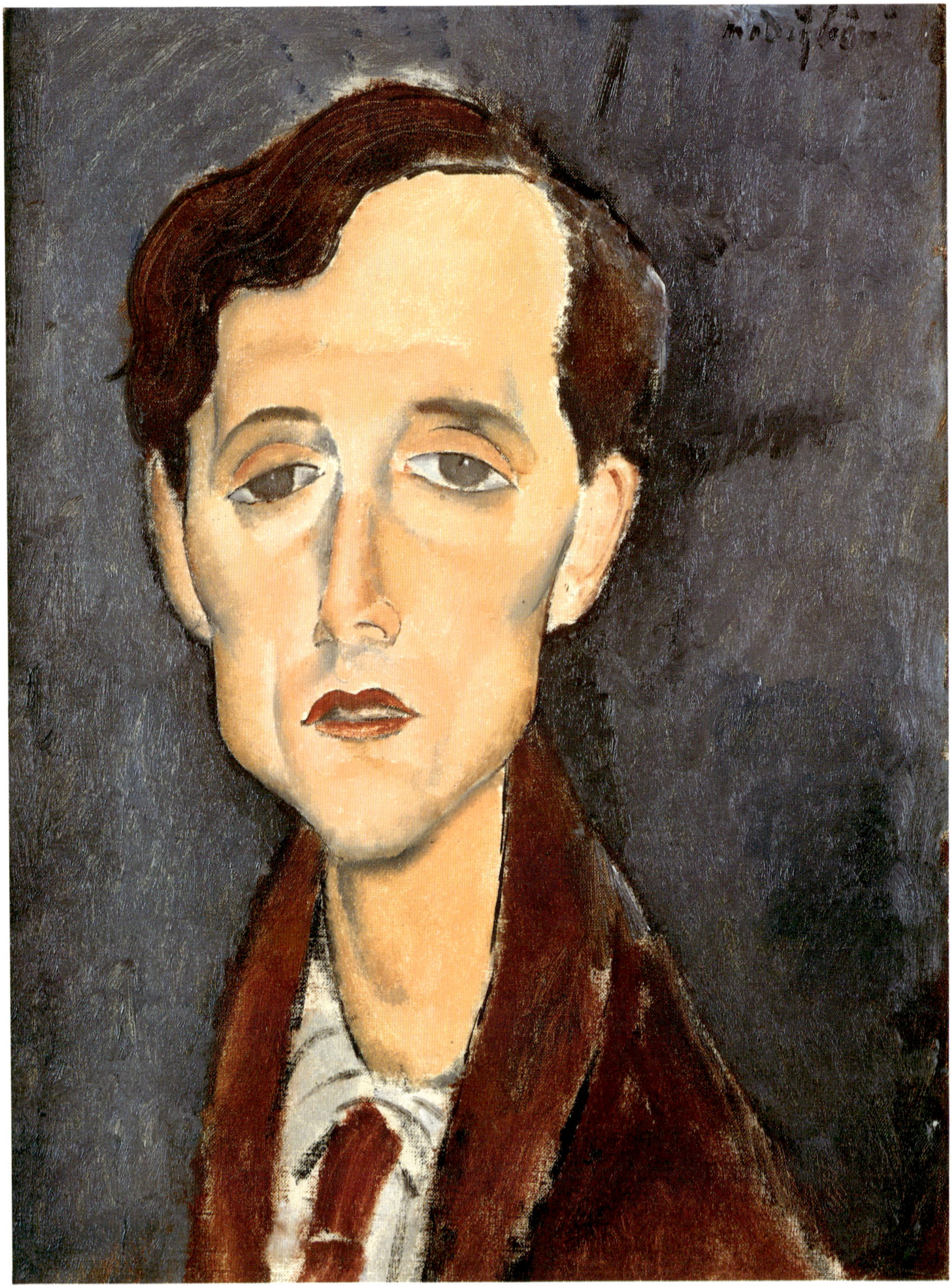

Portrait of Franz Hellens

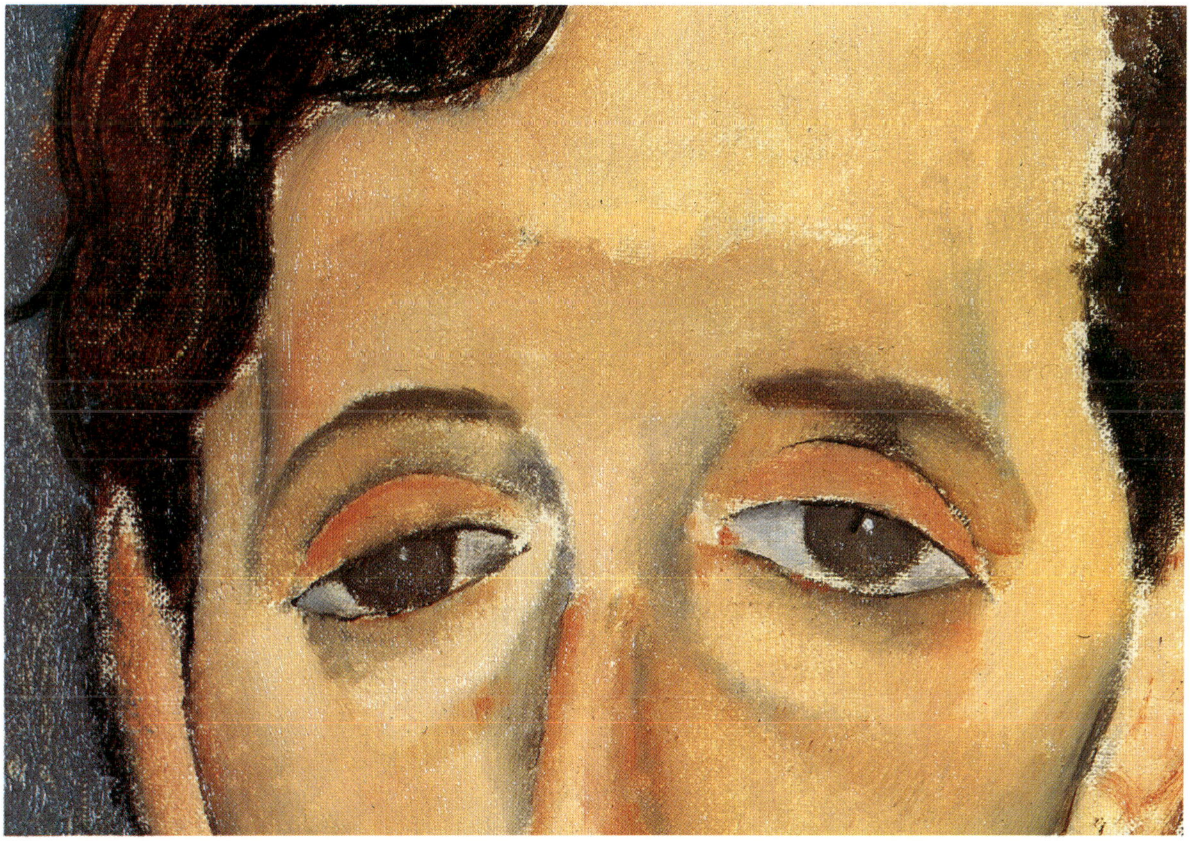

Portrait of Franz Hellens (Detail)

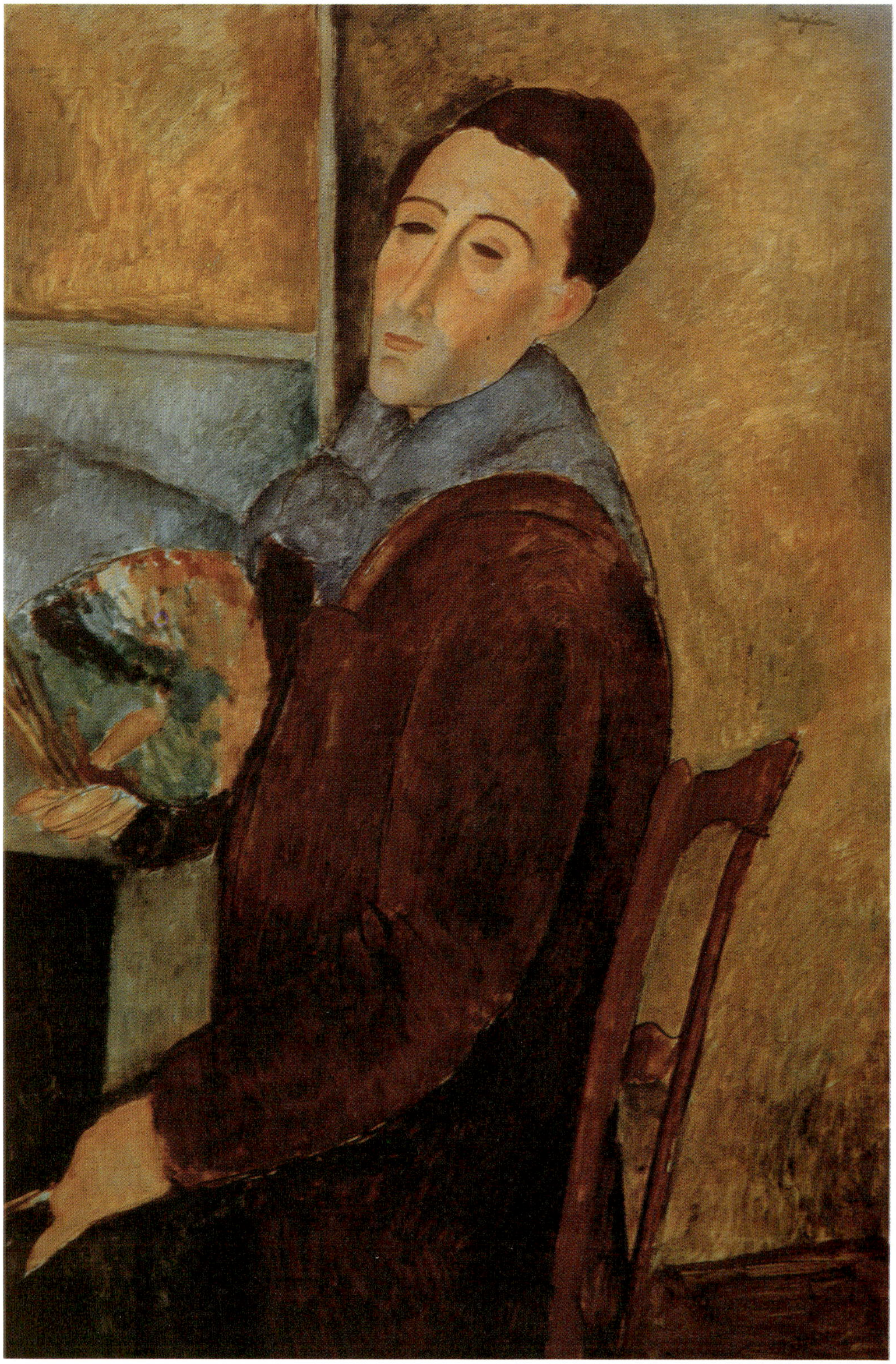

Self-Portrait

Stampa Grafiche Editoriali Padane Cremona